# Rhymes of Childhood

# Rhymes
# Of Childhood

By
## Edgar A. Guest

LIGHTYEAR PRESS

LAUREL, NEW YORK 11948

To

The Little Mother

who still watches through the window
to see me come,
this book is affectionately dedicated

# INDEX

Always Saying "Don't!" .............. 144
Another Mouth to Feed ............... 125
Answering Him ...................... 139
Approach of Christmas, The ........... 63
As It Goes .......................... 98
At Dawn ............................ 86
At Sixteen Months ................... 45
Aunty .............................. 104
Aw Gee Whiz! ....................... 168

Baby Feet .......................... 46
Baby in the House, A ................ 31
Bear Story, A ....................... 133
Being Brave at Night ................ 79
Boy and His Dad, A .................. 159
Boy and His Dog, A .................. 65
Boy and His Stomach, A .............. 53
Boy and the Flag, The ............... 50
Boy at Christmas, A ................. 109
Boy or Girl? ........................ 66
Boy's Hope for the Future, A ......... 161
Boy Soldier, The .................... 131
Broken Drum, The ................... 130
Bud Discusses Cleanliness ........... 88
Bumps and Bruises Doctor, The ....... 141

Castor Oil .......................... 85
Children, The ....................... 90
Choir Boy, The ...................... 174

# Index

Christmas Story, A...................... 21
Come Back, You Little Feller............ 33
Cookie-Lady, The ..................... 77
Couldn't Live Without You............. 162
Cut-Down Trousers, The.............. 111

Daddies ............................. 72
Different ............................ 106
Dinner-Time.......................... 83
Dirty Hands.......................... 185
Doctor, The.......................... 118
Dr. Johnson's Picture Cow............. 61

Fairy Story, A........................ 47
Fairy and the Robin, The.............. 179
Family Disgrace, The.................. 38
Feller's Hat, A....................... 149
Fine Sight, A......................... 108
Finest Age, The....................... 154
First Step, The........................ 24
Fractions ............................ 41
Fun of Forgiving, The................. 93

Good Little Boy, The.................. 153
Grandma ............................. 13
Grandpa ............................. 115
Grown Up ........................... 113

Habits .............................. 15
High Chair Days...................... 182
His Example ......................... 91
How the Baby Learned to Smile........ 11
Human Stage Coach, The.............. 42

I Don't Want to Go to Bed............. 101

# Index

Janet's Morning Bath.................. 37
Joy of a Dog, The..................... 137
Just a Boy............................ 18

Lanes of Boyhood, The................ 39
Last Night the Baby Cried............. 75
Leader of the Gang................... 164
Little Army, The..................... 128
Little Fishermen ..................... 76
Little Girls ......................... 82
Little Girls Are Best................. 165
Little Hurts, The..................... 112
Little Velvet Suit, The............... 120
Living Beauties, The.................. 170
Lullaby .............................. 54
Lure That Failed, The................ 126

Man to Be, The....................... 56
Morning Brigands..................... 102
My Paw Said So....................... 158

New Little Gimmie, The............... 19
No Children! ......................... 145
Nothing to Laugh At.................. 69

Old Wooden Tub, The................. 59
Our Son .............................. 32
Out-of-Doors ......................... 156

Pa Did It............................. 117
Path o' Little Children, The.......... 16
Pleasure's Signs...................... 81
Practicing Time....................... 150
Pretending Not to See................ 177

# Index

Real Swimming........................ 142
Rich ................................. 184
Right Family, The.................... 94
Rough Little Rascal, The.............. 44

Spoiler, The......................... 180
Spoiling Them........................ 122
Sticky Fingers ...................... 35
Story Telling........................ 171
Story Time........................... 123
Summer Children, The................ 58

Teach Them of the Flag............... 71
To a Little Girl..................... 147
Tonsils ............................. 96
To the Little Baby................... 176
Toy-Strewn Home, The................ 73

Up to the Ceiling.................... 138

"Wait Till Your Pa Comes Home"...... 67
Weaning the Baby..................... 23
What Home's Intended For............. 167
When a Little Baby Dies.............. 52
When Pa Comes Home................... 135
When There's Company for Tea........ 152
When the Soap Gets in Your Eye........ 99
When We Were Kids.................... 29
"Where's Mamma?".................... 49
Where the Children Meet............. 27
Wishing ............................. 26
Woe of an Unwilling Orator, The........ 20
World and Bud, The.................. 173

# Rhymes of Childhood

## How the Baby Learned to Smile

The first few weeks she never knew
The faces of the people who
Came flocking round her crib by day;
She looked at them the self-same way;
She treated all with cold disdain,
And recognized but hunger's pain.
We watched and wondered all the while
Just when our babe would learn to smile.

" She is too small," the mother said,
The while I stood above her bed
And hoped to see those big blue eyes
Light up with wonder and surprise.
" The world is all so strange and new,
She has not grown accustomed to
This curious earth, but by and by
You'll see a twinkle in her eye."

And then one morning when we woke
The mother looked at her and spoke,

And something marvelous took place —
A smile lit up the baby's face;
A smile! As radiant to see
As blossoms on a cherry tree!
A smile to us much brighter, far,
Than morning sun or evening star.

I fancy while that night we slept
An angel to her cradle crept
And touched those little lips and eyes
With brushes dipped in summer skies
And golden liquid from the sun,
And taught her how the smile is done.
At least I'm telling all the while
That's how our baby learned to smile.

# Grandma

I know what makes a Grandma grand — she
    always has a treat,
A cookie or a piece of cake or apple pie to eat,
And when we go to visit her she gets the good
    things out,
And we don't have to ask for more as long as
    she's about.
        Then Ma will say:
        " That's all to-day,
Don't give them any more;
        You'll make them ill,
        I know you will,
To-night we'll walk the floor."


A Grandma never punishes or says that we are
    bad,
She always takes us on her knee and tells us she
    is glad
To have us racing round the house, and when we
    get too smart,
An' Pa an' Ma are awful cross, she always takes
    our part.
        And once when I
        Had told a lie
And had to go to bed
        Without my tea,
        She came to me
And brought me jam and bread.

Ma says it's funny Grandma acts the way she
    does to-day;
When she was Grandma's little girl she couldn't
    disobey,
Or only eat the things she liked an' get the
    stomach ache,
Or pick the chocolate frosting off an' never touch
    the cake.
        When she was bad
        She always had
The punishment to bear,
        But we can be
        Much worse than she
An' Grandma doesn't care.

Pa says that Grandmas are alike; their job of
    training's done,
They don't like tears to come along and spoil the
    children's fun.
They love to see the youngsters eat, an', though
    it isn't right,
They never have to walk the floor or stay up all
    the night.
        An' children know
        The times they go
To Grandma's house to play,
        Though bad they are,
        Their Ma and Pa
Can't have a word to say.

## Habits

Habits are things which you do an' you
    shouldn't,
Things which a good little sissy boy wouldn't.
For instance, to sprawl on a bed in your clo'es,
An' yank off a shoe an' don't look where it goes,
An' take off a stocking an' give it a fling,
So that when it comes morning you can't find a
    thing
Which you know you took off.   It should be on
    the chair,
But habit has kept you from putting it there.

Habits are funny.   You do 'em, that's all,
And do 'em without ever thinking at all.
You say that you won't toss your hat on the floor,
Or bite down your nails till your fingers are sore,
Or sniffle your nose or sit humped in your chair
An' twist up an' play with a bunch of your hair;
An' you mean that you won't when you promise
    it then,
But the first thing you know you have done it
    again.

Habits are things that your parents detest,
Like twisting the button that's sewed on your
    vest,
Or scuffling your feet as you walk through the
    hall,

An' you don't even know that you do them at all.
You don't even know what's the matter when
    they
Bring you up with a jerk, with that: "Stop it,
    I say!"
Then they preach an' they talk an' they scold you
    a lot,
And it's all on account of that habit you've got.


## The Path o' Little Children

The path o' little children is the path I want to
    tread,
Where green is every valley and every rose is red,
Where laughter's always ringing and every smile
    is real,
And where the hurts are little hurts that just a
    kiss will heal.

The path o' little children, on the primrose edge
    of life,
That leads away from jealousy and bitterness and
    strife,

The path that leads to gladness — that's the way
    I want to go,
Where no one speaks unkindly and no one knows
    a foe.

The path o' little children that winds o'er hill
    and dale,
And leads us down to gentle seas where tiny
    vessels sail,
That takes us through the barnyard and through
    the pasture bars,
Will bring us home at evening with hearts that
    know no scars.

The path o' little children — there peaceful
    dreams come true,
There sunshine's always streaming and every sky
    is blue,
There each one loves the other, and every one
    is fair,
And cheeks are pink with beauty, and singing fills
    the air.

The path o' little children — it's there I want to
    tread,
Where innocence is dwelling with not a thing to
    dread,
Where care is not an ogre and sin is but a name
And no one thinks of money and no one sighs
    for fame.

## Just a Boy

He is just a boy with his eyes aglow,
Just a boy, and you love him so,
And his merry laugh and his roguish way
And those restless feet which turn to play
Are youth's rich treasures swiftly spent.
You had them once ere your boyhood went,
You raced and romped in the self-same way,
But you cry, "Keep still!" for you're tired
    to-day.

Time was you jeered at an easy chair
And an hour of quiet was hard to bear;
Then life was filled with a thousand things
And your arms and legs were strong as springs,
And the old folks said as they looked at you:
"He races and romps the whole day through,
And he's never tired and he can't sit still;
He ought to rest, but he never will."

He is just a boy, and a boy must jump,
And a boy must run till his pulses thump,
Must swing his arms and kick his heels
And give full vent to the joy he feels;
Must rush in the house and bolt his meals
And long for things which run on wheels;
And whenever you find him sitting still
It's not that he's tired — it's because he's ill.

# The New Little Gimme

There's a new little Gimme at our house,
  A new little Gimme who cries
For the silvery moon or a rattle or spoon,
  Or whatever is new to her eyes.
Though she's helpless and small, her old dad
    understands
Just what she means when she holds out her
    hands.

There's a new little Gimme at our house,
  A new little wanter of things,
Of ribbons and laces and bright jewel cases,
  Of watches and brooches and rings.
Though she's not one year old, in her feminine
    way
She knows how to get what she wants, day by
    day.

There's a new little Gimme at our house,
  A Gimme who's speechless, and yet
With a frown or a smile, what she wants for the
    while,
  Like her mother, she knows how to get.
With a grunt she demands, "Gimme this!
    Gimme that!"
Until sometimes her dad doesn't know where
    he's at.

There's a new little Gimme at our house,
   And though lovely and small she appears,
Her hands are held out for the joys round about
   And she gets them with smiles or with tears.
And her old dad declares that man's life and its
         whirl
Is lived just to give pretty things to a girl.

## The Woe of an Unwilling Orator

I wish I would get sick and couldn't go;
   I wish a fire would burn the school house
         down;
I wish we'd have at least ten feet of snow,
   So people couldn't get around the town;
I wish I'd get a black eye in a fight —
   I got to speak a piece to-morrow night.

I wish I'd lose my pants or get 'em torn;
   I hope that Ma can't find my shirt or hat
And, having nothing decent to be worn,
   She'll say: "I cannot let you go like that!"
But Ma will have my clothes laid out, all right —
   I got to speak a piece to-morrow night.

Some fellows can get sick and stay away;
  Sometimes the school house burns the night
    before;
Bill Green once broke his leg the very day
  He had to speak a piece, and Jimmy Moore
Tore out his Sunday pants right where he sat —
  But I don't ever have such luck as that.

Nothing I eat will make me sick to-day,
  I couldn't get a black eye if I tried;
Ma's got my Sunday clothes all put away;
  I wish I knew a place where I could hide.
But I'll be there, dressed up and frightened
    white —
  I got to speak a piece to-morrow night.

## A Christmas Story

Now, children, if you will just gather about,
I'll tell you the story of little Tom Doubt.
Just sit on the floor there and look up at me;
Yes, yes, I'll take two of you — one on each
    knee —

And now I'll begin.  Well, this little Tom Doubt
Said he couldn't figure old Santa Claus out.

He said that no reindeer could patter a hoof
Or gallop like mad on his snow-covered roof;
And he said that his chimney he knew was too
    small
For a white-whiskered saint to get down it at all,
And he didn't believe that the girls and the boys
From Santa Claus ever got candies and toys.

Now little Tom Doubt said: "I'll prove that
    I'm right;
No letter to Santa Claus this year I'll write.
I want a new sled and I want a new drum,
But I won't let him know that I want him to
    come.
I'll test out the Santa Claus story this year —
I won't even tell him that I'm living here."

When he woke in the morning, he found by his
    bed
The drum that he longed for, the new shiny sled,
And all that he wanted, yet never had told,
And his look of surprise was a joy to behold.
"Why, he's real! He has been here!" cried
    little Tom Doubt,
" But however did Santa Claus find all this out? "

## Weaning the Baby

Her tears are very near to-day,
    There's sorrow in her eyes,
For they have ordered her away
    Whene'er the baby cries.
There's little beauty in the sun
    However fair the day be,
For now the mother has begun
    The weaning of the baby.

No more upon her gentle breast
    That little face may lie,
No more that little nose be pressed
    Against her food supply;
No more by night, no more by day,
    That wondrous pleasure may be —
This shadow falls across the way,
    The weaning of the baby.

Oh, you may smile, but mother sighs,
    And now the hours are sad.
She sees the look of pained surprise
    In eyes that once were glad,
And in her throat a lump comes up
    That's big enough to throttle,
Because her lovely babe must sup
    Her dinner from a bottle.

Now bottles can't sing lullabies
   When tender babies dine,
Or read the love in little eyes
   When eagerly they shine.
And so she sadly says to me:
   "I'll miss her fond caresses,
The cuddling ways which used to be,
   Her tugging at my dresses.

"I'll miss her cry for me at night
   And all her squeals of glee,
Her smile of welcome and delight
   When she discovered me;
I'll miss the tie that holds me near
   And long will every day be,
I'm sorry that the time is here
   For me to wean the baby."

## The First Step

Last night she hurried out to say:
"The baby took a step to-day!"
A step alone!  Those little feet
Walked out two waiting hands to greet;

Walked boldly out, and left the chair
Which little hands had clung to there,

A very glorious hint to make
Of many steps she soon will take.

At eve they hurried out to say:
" The baby took a step to-day! "
What mattered letters, friendly calls,
And all the care which daily falls,
The news by 'phone, the gossip heard?
One thing important had occurred,
One big deed swept all else away:
The baby took a step to-day!

The baby took a step. Ah, me!
The first of millions that will be!
Those little feet will walk and climb
And run along the road of Time;
They've started out, and where they'll go
'Tis not permitted us to know.
Out of her arms she turns away —
The baby took a step to-day!

Dear Lord, now hear me as I pray.
Our baby took a step to-day!
Grant that her little feet shall find
No cruel pathways or unkind.
Be Thou her guide through life, that she
May walk in safe security.
Let love and beauty light her way —
Our baby took a step to-day!

# *Wishing*

I wisht my pa would ast me to
Do somefin 'at he wanted done;
I wisht he'd fink of somefin now
He needs, so's I could jump an' run
An' get it for him quick, so's he
Could see how good his boy can be.

I wisht my pa would say to me,
The way he's often done before,
" My 'baccy's gone.  Here, Willie, run
An' get some for me at the store."
I wisht he would, so's I could show
Him just how fast his boy can go.

I'm sittin' here jes' waitin' for
My pa to ast me now to get
His slippers an' his smokin' coat,
But he ain't ever ast me yet.
I wisht my pa would even say
" It's bed time " — I'd go right away.

I know 'at Christmus time is near
An' I would like my pa to see,
When he wants little errands done,
How willin' his own boy can be.
I wisht of somefin' he would fink —
I'd do it quicker'n a wink.

## Where the Children Meet

There's a little house on a humble street,
With a little porch where the children meet,
    And when school is out
    You can hear them shout,
An army glad, as they race about;
    To horn and drum
    They boldly come,
And they tramp the grass till it's brown and bare
    And the passers-by
    With a careful eye
Must watch for the wagons rolling there.

Now many a house on this street is prim,
With a grass plot neat and the windows trim,
    And a lovely sight
    Is the garden bright,
But it's all too fine for a paper fight;
    So the children go
    To a place they know,
Where the maid won't fly to the door and say:
    " Get out in the street
    With your dirty feet!
Don't you know that I washed that porch
      to-day?"

There is always a house on every street
That is known as the place where the children
    meet.
    You can pick it out
    As you walk about,
For it's there that the youngsters laugh and
    shout;
    And the grass is bare
    And the toys are there
And the wire fence sags where the lads have
    swung,
    And the paint is nicked
    Where their feet have kicked
And a window shows where a ball was flung.

And I think as I walk on that humble street,
Let mine be the house where the children meet;
    Let mine be the place
    Where they romp and race,
I can open that door with a smiling face.
    Let this army tramp
    In my yard, and camp
So long as they will, for the years roll on
    And the day draws near
    When the silence here
Will tell to the world that our babes have gone.

## When We Were Kids

When we wuz kids together, an' we didn't have
    a care,
In the lazy days of summer, when our feet wuz
    allus bare,
When a hat warn't necessary, an' a necktie in the
    way,
An' there warn't a blessed thing to do but scam-
    per off an' play,
Then the sun meant something to us, an' the blue
    skies overhead
Kinder stooped down in the meadows where the
    children wuz, and said:
" Trout are bitin' in the mill stream, hurry up an'
    git yer pole,
Now's the time you should be hikin' t' yer fav'rit
    fishin' hole."

When we wuz kids together, an' there warn't a
    thing t' fret,
'Cept comin' home to mother with our hair sus-
    picious wet,
Then the sunbeams an' the song birds used to
    come t' us an' say:
" They are swimmin' in th' river, better git there
    right away,
As we passed 'em we could hear 'em, laughin',
    splashin' down below."

Then we hurried to the river, just as fast as we
could go,
For there warn't a thing to keep us like there is
now we are men,
An' the sunbeams an' the song birds an' the skies
meant somethin' then.

Now the same sunbeams come callin', an' the
same song birds come near,
An' the same blue skies bend o'er me an' their
messages I hear;
Every dancing sunbeam tells me that out yonder
in the stream
Now the pickerel are bitin', but I only sit an'
dream,
For I've journeyed past my boyhood, I'm a slave
forevermore,
An' I must not heed their whispers as I used to
do of yore.
There are bills to meet and duties that I must not,
dare not shirk;
Mr. Sunbeam, quit yer coaxin', it's no use, I've
got to work.

# A Baby in the House

Something to talk about, something to do,
Something to laugh at the whole day through,
Something to look at with pride and with glee,
Something for friends to come in just to see;
Oh, you can't sum up all the wonderful things
Of joy and delight which a new baby brings.

There's a smile that is brighter than sunbeams
    of May,
A wave of farewell as you're starting away,
A glad time of frolic which no one can steal,
A thrill inexpressible, lovely to feel.
There's something to boast of and something to
    tell
When a baby has come to the place where you
    dwell.

There's never an hour that is lonely and drear;
The days are filled up to the top with good cheer.
You have someone to play with and someone to
    sing to,
Someone to romp with and someone to cling to;
And always you're finding some pleasure that's
    new
When God has sent down a glad baby to you.

## Our Son

He's supposed to be our son, our hope and our
    pride,
In him all the dreams of our future abide,
But whenever some act to his credit occurs
I never am mentioned, the glory is hers,
And whenever he's bad or has strayed from the
    line,
Then always she speaks of the rascal as mine.

When trouble has come she will soberly say:
"Do you know what *your* son has been up to
    to-day?
*Your* son spilled the ink on the living room floor!
*Your* son broke the glass in the dining room door!
I am telling you now something has to be done,
It is high time you started correcting *your* son!"

But when to the neighbors she boasts of his
    worth,
It is: " My son's the best little boy on the
    earth!"
Accuse him of mischief, she'll just floor you flat
With: " My son, I'm certain, would never do
    that!
Of course there are times when he's wilfully bad.
But then it's that temper he gets from his dad!"

## Come Back, You Little Feller

Come back, you little feller, come back again
    to me,
To walk the shady lanes once more and sail the
    golden sea;
Come back unto your daddy, for I'm longing so
    to-day
To tread the paths of boyhood and to live the
    joys of May.
Come back, you little feller, for my heart is
    aching so;
Come back to go a-strolling where the checker-
    berries grow.

Come back, you little feller; Oh, my heart is
    crying now,
Come back, come back with laughter and the sun-
    shine on your brow;
Come back to cheer your daddy and we'll romp
    the world along;
We'll scamper through the pasture and we'll sing
    a merry song;
We'll roam the apple orchard and we'll hunt the
    honey bees;
Come back to soothe your daddy, for my heart
    is ill at ease.

Come back, you little feller, for to-day your
daddy strolled
Alone along the pathways where we used to hunt
for gold.
Not a fairy came to cheer me, not an elfin laughed
in glee,
Though I sought the self-same places where they
always used to be;
And the song birds in the tree tops seemed to
sing as if they knew
That my aching heart was calling, ever calling
loud for you.

Come back, you little feller, don't you hear your
daddy cry,
Don't you hear him nightly pleading, don't you
hear his bitter sigh?
For I'm lonely here without you, and the fields
are lonely, too,
And the days have lost their sunshine and the
skies are never blue.
So I wander through the meadows and the fields
we used to roam,
While my heart is ever calling, "Little feller,
come back home."

## Sticky Fingers

Little sticky fingers, it is very plain to see
With your pulling and your tugging that you
    make a wreck of me.
    There's a splotch upon my collar
    That is larger than a dollar,
And my new and costly necktie is a positive
    disgrace!
    On the bosom of my shirt
    You have left a smear of dirt,
And something seems to tell me there is butter
    on my face.

Little sticky fingers, what's a grown-up man to do
When he comes down stairs o' mornings to a
    laughing babe like you,
    And your arms are held out, shaking
    For a bit of merry-making,
And those chubby little fingers and those rosy
    little thumbs
    Seem to dance and throb with glee?
    Would any daddy flee
To save his spotless collar from the butter and
    the crumbs?

Little sticky fingers, as a gentleman is dressed
I have held you on my shoulder and I've hugged
    you to my breast,

While those little hands were pressing
All the signs of their caressing
On my white and shining raiment, and I've seen
the people smile
At my collar sadly soiled
Where your rosy thumbs had moiled —
But linen doesn't matter, it is only pomp and
style.

Little sticky fingers, stamp your seals of love
on me;
Press those hands upon my collar and it's happy
I will be.
Oh, it's little I am caring
For the linen I am wearing,
I would rather own those smudges than the jewels
of a king;
I would rather folks could see
Every stain you leave on me
Than to wear a spotless collar where no sticky
fingers cling.

## Janet's Morning Bath

I've seen some lovely sights, I think —
A rosebud bursting into pink,
A distant hill top drenched with gold,
A tree with all that it could hold
Of blossoms in the early spring —
But there can be no lovelier thing
Among the beauties Nature hath
Than little Janet in her bath.

Come upstairs now with me and see
Our baby on her mother's knee,
And watch this glad performance through —
A pretty sight I'll show to you!
Fairer than any landscape scene
Or silver brook or meadow green,
I'll show you dimpled legs and arms
And babyhood with all its charms.

I'm sorry for the man who hath
Not seen a baby in her bath,
For be he old and be he wise,
He does not know the charm which lies
In tiny bodies, plump and sweet
And little toes on rosy feet;
Nor does he know how fair to see
A baby in her bath can be.

# The Family Disgrace

Whenever I come where the old folks is,
" Jes' look at your hands," says Ma;
And Sis says " My!" though it's none of her biz,
" An' look at his neck," says Pa.
"An' look at the mud on his stockings, too,
An' look at his dirty face,
It ain't a week since his shoes were new!"
   Oh, it's awful tough when you know that you
   Are the family's one disgrace.

" Jes' look how the seat of his pants is worn!
Did you ever see such hair?
An' that is his very best blouse that's torn,
An' his coat's got another tear.
He might be a rag picker's boy," says Ma,
" The alley's about his place."
" He ought to be spanked, that's what," says Pa.
   Oh, it's awful tough when you know that
     you are
   The family's one disgrace.

" Now what's he got in his pockets, pray?
An' where does he get such things?
An' why does he bulge out his clothes that way
With marbles an' tops an' strings?
Don't you dare to sit down till you've been up
     stairs

An' scrubbed both your hands an' your face,
My goodness! Don't handle those portieres!"
   Oh, nobody loves an' nobody cares
   For the family's one disgrace.


### The Lanes of Boyhood

Down the lanes of boyhood let me go once more,
Let me tread the paths of youth that I have trod
      before;
Let me wander once again where the skies are
      bright,
Freckled faced and tanned of leg, roadways of
      delight,
Picking checkerberries as I laze along the way,
Hunting for the robin's nest, dozing in the hay.

Down the lanes of boyhood there are joys untold.
Hidden caves of precious things, stores of yellow
      gold,
Friends that only boyhood knows, birds and trees
      and flowers,
Nodding to the youngsters "Howdy do" in
      morning hours,

Skies that bend above them in the gentlest sort
of way,
Fleecy clouds that seem to stop and watch them
at their play.

Down the lanes of boyhood, hear their laughter
ring;
See the tousled army marching straightway to
the spring!
Flat upon the ground they fall, just to get a
drink;
Here's a thirst emporium where glasses never
clink.
No glittering place of red and gold the passer-by
to snare,
Yet rich with Nature's coloring, a thousand times
more rare.

Down the lanes of boyhood, where innocence
abounds,
A medley of colors, a revelry of sounds,
Where hearts are never broken and wrong is
never known,
Where sorrow never enters and no one weeps
alone.
And yet we never can return when once we've
journeyed on;
Old age is ever wishing for the joys forever
gone.

# Fractions

I hadn't asked about it for a week or two, and so
The stage of his arithmetic I really didn't know;
I had watched him through addition and division
  and the rest,
But I wasn't really certain just how far he had
  progressed
Till I saw him sitting, troubled and, I knew it
  from his actions,
From the way he chewed his pencil, that he'd
  journeyed into fractions.

He sprawled upon the table, and he twisted in
  his chair,
He sat and fumbled sadly with a tangled lock of
  hair;
He muttered and he sputtered and he gazed
  about the room,
A puzzled little fellow in a cloud of darkest
  gloom.
Then I softly asked him: "Sonny, what's the
  cause of these distractions?"
And he shook his head and answered: "Aw,
  gee whiz! We're into fractions!"

Oh, the time was I was like him; once I wore
  that troubled look,
Once I chewed my bit of pencil and I fumbled
  with the book,

Once I sprawled upon the table and was flounder-
    ing about
In a labyrinth of darkness and a dreadful mire
    of doubt;
And I chuckled as I  saw him reproduce my
    troubled actions
When my youthful head was bothered by the
    mystery of fractions.


## The Human Stage Coach

Twenty times a day we go
Round about the room just so,
Stopping here to watch the clock,
Pausing here a chair to rock,
Standing here to see the light
On and off, now dark, now bright,
Here to watch the sunbeams creep
On a painted flock of sheep.

Here's a merry round to make,
Here's a wonder-ride to take!
Same old glorious sights to view,
Never changed, but always new.

Starting at the clock we go
To the joys she's learned to know;
She's the driver, I'm the stage,
Bound for the canary cage.

Nothing must be missed at all,
On the shelf or on the wall,
This old battered coach must make
Every stop for pleasure's sake.
"Oo!" she cries, and that's a hint
Something she would finger-print,
Wheresoever we have been
There her thumb marks may be seen.

Which is happier, driver — stage,
Babyhood or gray-haired age?
Well, her smiles are fair to see,
But the coach I'm proud to be,
Glad that I can make the trip
Out and back without a slip,
Proud to be her daily stage
Bound for the canary cage.

# The Rough Little Rascal

A smudge on his nose and a smear on his cheek
And knees that might not have been washed in
    a week;
A bump on his forehead, a scar on his lip,
A relic of many a tumble and trip:
A rough little, tough little rascal, but sweet,
Is he that each evening I'm eager to meet.

A brow that is beady with jewels of sweat;
A face that's as black as a visage can get;
A suit that at noon was a garment of white,
Now one that his mother declares is a fright:
A fun-loving, sun-loving rascal, and fine,
Is he that comes placing his black fist in mine.

A crop of brown hair that is tousled and tossed;
A waist from which two of the buttons are lost;
A smile that shines out through the dirt and the
    grime,
And eyes that are flashing delight all the time:
All these are the joys that I'm eager to meet
And look for the moment I get to my street.

## At Sixteen Months

At sixteen months, when they start to walk,
And a few brief words is their sum of talk,
When their smile is a marvelous joy to see
And they want to ride on their daddy's knee,
When you get tired but they never do — *
For everything in this world is new —
It's then, I say, that a baby pays
For all of her care in her helpless days.

At sixteen months, when they crow with glee
And their arms reach up for the things they see,
When a smile breaks out on that cherub face
The minute you call from your hiding place,
When you know how the worst of you spoils
    your worth
But to her you're the greatest man on earth,
It's then, I say, that you're downright glad
The good Lord chose you to be a dad.

At sixteen months, let me say to you,
There's a thrill in everything babies do.
They'll keep you going and wear you out,
They'll cling to your hand as you walk about,
But you'll laugh and sing and boast your fill
Of your marvelous baby. Oh, yes, you will!
For at sixteen months, I am here to state,
Every baby, in spite of its dad, is great.

## Baby Feet

Tell me, what is half so sweet
As a baby's tiny feet,
Pink and dainty as can be,
Like a coral from the sea?
Talk of jewels strung in rows,
Gaze upon those little toes,
Fairer than a diadem,
With the mother kissing them!

It is morning and she lies
Uttering her happy cries,
While her little hands reach out
For the feet that fly about.
Then I go to her and blow
Laughter out of every toe;
Hold her high and let her place
Tiny footprints on my face.

Little feet that do not know
Where the winding roadways go,
Little feet that never tire,
Feel the stones or trudge the mire,
Still too pink and still too small
To do anything but crawl,
Thinking all their wanderings fair,
Filled with wonders everywhere.

Little feet, so rich with charm,
May you never come to harm.
As I bend and proudly blow
Laughter out of every toe,
This I pray, that God above
Shall protect you with His love,
And shall guide those little feet
Safely down life's broader street.


## *A Fairy Story*

Sit here on my knee, little girl, and I'll tell
      A story to you
      Of a fairy I knew
Who lived in a garden when I was a child.
She was lovely to see and whenever she smiled
The sunbeams came dancing around just to know
Whatever it was that was pleasing her so.

She lived in a poppy and used to peek out
      And shout: "Oh, Yoo-hoo!
      I've been waiting for you!"
And then I'd go over to her house and play
And she'd saddle a bee and we'd both ride away,
Or sometimes we'd take a most wonderful trip
With the sky for the sea and a cloud for our
      ship.

47

Oft my father and mother would look out and
        say:
        " The glad little elf
        Plays there all by himself,
And he comes in and tells us of things he has
        seen
And the marvelous places to which he has been;
He tells us of dining with princes and kings —
It's a curious boy who can think up such things."

Now this all occurred in the long years ago,
        And the fairy has fled,
        And the poppies are dead,
And never again may I ride on a bee,
Or sail on a cloud with the sky for the sea.
But that fairy has promised, when poppies are
        fair,
To come back again and to wait for you there.

Yes, you can go out when the skies are all blue
        And see what I've seen,
        And go where I've been.
You can have the fairies to lead you away,
To show you strange sights and to share in your
        play;
And the grown-ups may say that your fancies
        are wild,
But fairies are real to an innocent child.

## " Where's Mamma? "

Comes in flying from the street:
    " Where's Mamma? "
Friend or stranger thus he'll greet:
    " Where's Mamma? "
Doesn't want to say hello,
Home from school or play he'll go
Straight to what he wants to know:
    " Where's Mamma? "

Many times a day he'll shout,
    " Where's Mamma? "
Seems afraid that she's gone out;
    " Where's Mamma? "
Is his first thought at the door —
She's the one he's looking for,
And he questions o'er and o'er,
    " Where's Mamma? "

Can't be happy till he knows:
    " Where's Mamma? "
So he begs us to disclose
    " Where's Mamma? "
And it often seems to me,
As I hear his anxious plea,
That no sweeter phrase can be:
    " Where's Mamma? "

Like to hear it day by day:
   "Where's Mamma?"
Loveliest phrase that lips can say:
   "Where's Mamma?"
And I pray as time shall flow,
And the long years come and go,
That he'll always want to know
   "Where's Mamma?"


## The Boy and the Flag

I want my boy to love his home,
  His Mother, yes, and me:
I want him, wheresoe'er he'll roam,
  With us in thought to be.
I want him to love what is fine,
  Nor let his standards drag,
But, Oh! I want that boy of mine
  To love his country's flag!

I want him when he older grows
  To love all things of earth;
And Oh! I want him, when he knows,
  To choose the things of worth.

I want him to the heights to climb
  Nor let ambition lag;
But, Oh! I want him all the time
  To love his country's flag.


I want my boy to know the best,
  I want him to be great;
I want him in Life's distant West,
  Prepared for any fate.
I want him to be simple, too,
  Though clever, ne'er to brag,
But, Oh! I want him, through and through,
  To love his country's flag.


I want my boy to be a man,
  And yet, in distant years,
I pray that he'll have eyes that can
  Not quite keep back the tears
When, coming from some foreign shore
  And alien scenes that fag,
Borne on its native breeze, once more
  He sees his country's flag.

## When a Little Baby Dies

When a little baby dies
And the wee form silent lies,
And the little cheeks seem waxen
And the little hands are still,
Then your soul gives way to treason,
And you cry: " O, God, what reason,
O, what justice and what mercy
Have You shown us by Your will?

" Oh, there are so many here
Of the yellow leaf and sere,
Who are anxious, aye, and ready
To respond unto Your call;
Yet You pass them by unheeding,
And You set our hearts to bleeding!
Oh how bitterly upon us
Do Your vaunted mercies fall!"

Yet some day, in after years,
When Death's angel once more nears,
And the unknown, silent river
Looms as darkly as a pall,
You will hear your baby saying,
" Mamma, come to me, I'm staying
With my arms outstretched to greet you,"
And you'll understand it all.

## A Boy and His Stomach

What's the matter with you — ain't I always
    been your friend?
Ain't I been a pardner to you? All my pennies
    don't I spend
In gettin' nice things for you? Don't I give
    you lots of cake?
Say, stummick, what's the matter, that you had
    to go an' ache?

Why, I loaded you with good things; yesterday
    I gave you more
Potatoes, squash an' turkey than you'd ever had
    before.
I gave you nuts an' candy, pumpkin pie an'
    chocolate cake,
An' las' night when I got to bed you had to
    go an' ache.

Say, what's the matter with you — ain't you
    satisfied at all?
I gave you all you wanted, you was hard jes'
    like a ball,
An' you couldn't hold another bit of puddin',
    yet las' night
You ached mos' awful, stummick; that ain't
    treatin' me jes' right.

I've been a friend to you, I have, why ain't you
a friend o' mine?
They gave me castor oil last night because you
made me whine.
I'm awful sick this mornin' an' I'm feelin' mighty
blue,
Because you don't appreciate the things I do for
you.

## Lullaby

The golden dreamboat's ready, all her silken sails
are spread,
And the breeze is gently blowing to the fairy
port of Bed,
And the fairy captain's waiting while the busy
sandman flies
With the silver dust of slumber, closing every
baby's eyes.

Oh, the night is rich with moonlight and the sea
is calm with peace,
And the angels fly to guard you and their watch
shall never cease,

And the fairies there await you; they have splendid dreams to spin;
You shall hear them gayly singing as the dreamboat's putting in.

Like the ripple of the water does the dreamboat's
   whistle blow,
Only baby ears can catch it when it comes the
   time to go,
Only little ones may journey on so wonderful a
   ship,
And go drifting off to slumber with no care to
   mar the trip.

Oh, the little eyes are heavy but the little soul is
   light;
It shall never know a sorrow or a terror through
   the night.
And at last when dawn is breaking and the
   dreamboat's trip is o'er,
You shall wake to find the mother smiling over
   you once more.

## The Man to Be

Some day the world will need a man of courage
    in a time of doubt,
And somewhere, as a little boy, that future hero
    plays about.
Within some humble home, no doubt, that instru-
    ment of greater things
Now climbs upon his father's knee or to his
    mother's garments clings
And when shall come that call for him to render
    service that is fine,
He that shall do God's mission here may be your
    little boy or mine.

Long years of preparation mark the pathway for
    the splendid souls,
And generations live and die and seem no nearer
    to their goals,
And yet the purpose of it all, the fleeting pleasure
    and the woe,
The laughter and the grief of life that all who
    come to earth must know
May be to pave the way for one — one man to
    serve the Will Divine
And it is possible that he may be your little boy
    or mine.

Some day the world will need a man! I stand
    beside his cot at night
And wonder if I'm teaching him, as best I can,
    to know the right.
I am the father of a boy — his life is mine to
    make or mar —
For he no better can become than what my daily
    teachings are;
There will be need for someone great — I dare
    not falter from the line —
The man that is to serve the world may be that
    little boy of mine.

Perhaps your boy or mine may not ascend the
    lofty heights of fame;
The orders for their births are hid. We know
    not why to earth they came;
Yet in some little bed to-night the great man of
    to-morrow sleeps
And only He who sent him here, the secret of
    His purpose keeps.
As fathers then our care is this — to keep in mind
    the Great Design —
The man the world shall need some day may be
    your little boy or mine.

# The Summer Children

I like 'em in the winter when their cheeks are
    slightly pale,
I like 'em in the spring time when the March
    winds blow a gale;
But when summer suns have tanned 'em and
    they're racing to and fro,
I somehow think the children make the finest
    sort of show.

When they're brown as little berries and they're
    bare of foot and head,
And they're on the go each minute where the
    velvet lawns are spread,
Then their health is at its finest and they never
    stop to rest,
Oh, it's then I think the children look and are
    their very best.

We've got to know the winter and we've got to
    know the spring,
But for children, could I do it, unto summer I
    would cling;
For I'm happiest when I see 'em, as a wild and
    merry band
Of healthy, lusty youngsters that the summer
    sun has tanned.

# The Old Wooden Tub

I like to get to thinking of the old days that are
  gone,
When there were joys that never more the world
  will look upon,
The days before inventors smoothed the little
  cares away
And made, what seemed but luxuries then, the
  joys of every day;
When bathrooms were exceptions, and we got
  our weekly scrub
By standing in the middle of a little wooden
  tub.

We had no rapid heaters, and no blazing gas to
  burn,
We boiled the water on the stove, and each one
  took his turn.
Sometimes to save expenses we would use one
  tub for two;
The water brother Billy used for me would
  also do,
Although an extra kettle I was granted, I admit,
On winter nights to freshen and to warm it up
  a bit.

We carried water up the stairs in buckets and
   in pails,
And sometimes splashed it on our legs, and rent
   the air with wails,
But if the nights were very cold, by closing every
   door
We were allowed to take our bath upon the
   kitchen floor.
Beside the cheery stove we stood and gave our-
   selves a rub,
In comfort most luxurious in that old wooden
   tub.

But modern homes no more go through that joyous weekly fun,
And through the sitting rooms at night no half-
   dried children run;
No little flying forms go past, too swift to see
   their charms,
With shirts and underwear and things tucked
   underneath their arms;
The home's so full of luxury now, it's almost like
   a club,
I sometimes wish we could go back to that old
   wooden tub.

## Dr. Johnson's Picture Cow

Got a sliver in my hand
An' it hurt t' beat the band,
An' got white around it, too;
Then the first thing that I knew
It was all swelled up, an' Pa
Said: "There's no use fussin', Ma,
Jes' put on his coat an' hat;
Doctor Johnson must see that."

I was scared an' yelled, because
One time when the doctor was
At our house he made me smell
Something funny, an' I fell
Fast asleep, an' when I woke
Seemed like I was goin' t' choke;
An' the folks who stood about
Said I'd had my tonsils out.

An' my throat felt awful sore
An' I couldn't eat no more,
An' it hurt me when I'd talk,
An' they wouldn't let me walk.
So when Pa said I must go
To the doctor's, I said: "No,
I don't want to go to-night,
'Cause my hand will be all right."

61

Pa said, " Take him, Ma," an' so
I jes' knew I had t' go.
An' the doctor looked an' said:
" It is very sore an' red —
Much too sore to touch at all.
See that picture on the wall,
That one over yonder, Bud,
With the old cow in the mud?

" Once I owned a cow like that,
Jes' as brown an' big an' fat,
An' one day I pulled her tail
An' she kicked an' knocked the pail
Full o' milk clean over me."
Then I looked up there t' see
His old cow above the couch,
An' right then I hollered 'ouch.' "

" Bud," says he, " what's wrong with **you;**
Did the old cow kick you, too? "
An' he laughed, an' Ma said:  " Son,
Never mind, now, it's all done."
Pretty soon we came away
An' my hand's all well to-day.
But that's first time that I knew
Picture cows could kick at you.

## The Approach of Christmas

There's a little chap at our house that is being
  mighty good —
Keeps the front lawn looking tidy in the way
  we've said he should;
Doesn't leave his little wagon, when he's finished
  with his play,
On the sidewalk as he used to; now he puts it
  right away.
When we call him in to supper, we don't have to
  stand and shout;
It is getting on to Christmas and it's plain he's
  found it out.

He eats the food we give him without murmur
  or complaint;
He sits up at the table like a cherub or a saint;
He doesn't pinch his sister just to hear how loud
  she'll squeal;
Doesn't ask us to excuse him in the middle of
  the meal,
And at eight o'clock he's willing to be tucked
  away in bed.
It is getting close to Christmas; nothing further
  need be said.

I chuckle every evening as I see that little elf,
With the crooked part proclaiming that he
    brushed his hair himself.
And I chuckle as I notice that his hands and face
    are clean,
For in him a perfect copy of another boy is
    seen —
A little boy at Christmas, who was also being
    good,
Never guessing that his father and his mother
    understood.

There's a little boy at our house that is being
    mighty good;
Doing everything that's proper, doing everything
    he should.
But besides him there's a grown-up who has
    learned life's bitter truth,
Who is gladly living over all the joys of vanished
    youth.
And although he little knows it (for it's what I
    never knew),
There's a mighty happy father sitting at the table,
    too.

## A Boy and His Dog

A boy and his dog make a glorious pair:
No better friendship is found anywhere,
For they talk and they walk and they run and
    they play,
And they have their deep secrets for many a
    day;
And that boy has a comrade who thinks and
    who feels,
Who walks down the road with a dog at his
    heels.

He may go where he will and his dog will be
    there,
May revel in mud and his dog will not care;
Faithful he'll stay for the slightest command
And bark with delight at the touch of his hand;
Oh, he owns a treasure which nobody steals,
Who walks down the road with a dog at his
    heels.

No other can lure him away from his side;
He's proof against riches and station and pride;
Fine dress does not charm him, and flattery's
    breath
Is lost on the dog, for he's faithful to death;
He sees the great soul which the body conceals —
And it's great to be young with a dog at your
    heels!

# Boy or Girl?

Some folks pray for a boy, and some
For a golden-haired little girl to come.
  Some claim to think there is more of joy
  Wrapped up in the smile of a little boy,
  While others pretend that the silky curls
  And plump, pink cheeks of the little girls
  Bring more of bliss to the old home place
  Than a small boy's queer little freckled face.

Now which is better, I couldn't say
If the Lord should ask me to choose to-day;
  If He should put in a call for me
  And say: " Now what shall your order be,
  A boy or girl?  I have both in store —
  Which of the two are you waiting for?"
  I'd say with one of my broadest grins:
  " Send either one, if it can't be twins."

I've heard it said, to some people's shame,
They cried with grief when a small boy came,
  For they wanted a girl.  And some folks I
    know
  Who wanted a boy, just took on so
  When a girl was sent.  But it seems to me
  That mothers and fathers should happy be
  To think, when the Stork has come and gone,
  That the Lord would trust them with either
    one.

Boy or girl?  There can be no choice;
There's something lovely in either voice.
   And all that I ask of the Lord to do
   Is to see that the mother comes safely through
   And guard the baby and have it well,
   With a perfect form and a healthy yell,
   And a pair of eyes and a shock of hair.
   Then, boy or girl — and its dad won't care.


## "*Wait Till Your Pa Comes Home*"

"Wait till your Pa comes home!"  Oh, dear!
What a dreadful threat for a boy to hear.
Yet never a boy of three or four
But has heard it a thousand times or more.
"Wait till your Pa comes home, my lad,
And see what you'll get for being bad.

"Wait till your Pa comes home, you scamp!
You've soiled the walls with your fingers damp,
You've tracked the floor with your muddy feet
And fought with the boy across the street;
You've torn your clothes and you look a sight!
But wait til your Pa comes home to-night."
Now since I'm the Pa of that daily threat
Which paints me as black as a thing of jet

I rise in protest right here to say
I won't be used in so fierce a way;
No child of mine in the evening gloam
Shall be afraid of my coming home.

I want him waiting for me at night
With eyes that glisten with real delight;
When it's right that punished my boy should be
I don't want the job postponed for me;
I want to come home to a round of joy
And not to frighten a little boy.

" Wait till your Pa comes home!"  Oh, dear,
What a dreadful threat for a boy to hear.
Yet that is ever his Mother's way
Of saving herself from a bitter day;
And well she knows in the evening gloam
He won't be hurt when his Pa comes home.

## Nothing to Laugh At

'Tain't nothin' to laugh at as I can see!
If you'd been stung by a bumble bee,
An' your nose wuz swelled an' it smarted, too,
You wouldn't want people to laugh at you.
If you had a lump that wuz full of fire,
Like you'd been touched by a red hot wire,
An' your nose spread out like a load of hay,
You wouldn't want strangers who come your
    way
To ask you to let 'em see the place
An' laugh at you right before your face.

What's funny about it, I'd like to know?
It isn't a joke to be hurted so!
An' how wuz I ever on earth to tell
'At the pretty flower which I stooped to smell
In our back yard wuz the very one
Which a bee wuz busily working on?
An' jus' as I got my nose down there,
He lifted his foot an' kicked for fair,
An' he planted his stinger right into me —
But it's nothin' to laugh at as I can see.

I let out a yell an' my Maw came out
To see what the trouble wuz all about.

She says from my shriek she wuz sure 'at I
Had been struck by a motor car passin' by;
But when she found what the matter wuz
She laughed just like ever'body does
An' she made me stand while she poked about
To pull his turrible stinger out.
An' my Pa laughed, too, when he looked at me —
But it's nothin' to laugh at, as I can see.

My Maw put witch-hazel on the spot
To take down the swellin', but it has not.
It seems to git bigger as time goes by
An' I can't see good out o' this one eye;
An' it hurts clean down to my very toes
Whenever I've got to blow my nose.
An' all I can say is when this gits well
There ain't any flowers I'll stoop to smell.
I'm through disturbin' a bumble bee —
But it's nothin' to laugh at, as I can see.

## Teach Them of the Flag

Teach the children of the Flag,
   Let them know the joy it holds
   In its sun-kissed rippling folds;
Don't let patriotism lag:
   Train them so that they will love
   Every star and stripe above.

As you teach their lips to pray,
   Teach them always to be true
   To the red, the white and blue;
Praise the Flag from day to day,
   Tell the children at your knee
   All the joys of liberty.

Let them know and understand
   How the Flag was born and why;
   Tell how brave men went to die
Gladly for their native land;
   Whisper to them that they must
   Make the Flag their sacred trust.

Love of country ever starts
   In the home and at your knee;
   There the Flag shall come to be
Shrined in patriotic hearts;
   They shall gladly serve their land
   When they know and understand.

## Daddies

I would rather be the daddy
  Of a romping, roguish crew,
Of a bright-eyed chubby laddie
  And a little girl or two,
Than the monarch of a nation,
  In his high and lofty seat,
Taking empty adoration
  From the subjects at his feet.

I would rather own their kisses,
  As at night to me they run,
Than to be the king who misses
  All the simpler forms of fun.
When his dreary day is ending
  He is dismally alone,
But when my sun is descending
  There are joys for me to own.

He may ride to horns and drumming,
  I must walk a quiet street;
But when once they see me coming,
  Then on joyous, flying feet
They come racing to me madly
  And I catch them with a swing,
And I say it proudly, gladly,
  That I'm happier than a king.

You may talk of lofty places;
　　You may boast of pomp and power;
Men may turn their eager faces
　　To the glory of an hour,
But give me the humble station
　　With its joys that long survive,
For the daddies of the nation
　　Are the happiest men alive.


## The Toy-Strewn Home

Give me the house where the toys are strewn,
　　Where the dolls are asleep in the chairs,
Where the building blocks and the toy balloon
　　And the soldiers guard the stairs.
Let me step in a house where the tiny cart
　　With the horses rules the floor,
And rest comes into my weary heart,
　　For I am at home once more.

Give me the house with the toys about,
　　With the battered old train of cars,
The box of paints and the books left out,
　　And the ship with her broken spars.

Let me step in a house at the close of day
  That is littered with children's toys,
And dwell once more in the haunts of play,
  With the echoes of by-gone noise.

Give me the house where the toys are seen,
  The house where the children romp,
And I'll happier be than man has been
  'Neath the gilded dome of pomp.
Let me see the litter of bright-eyed play
  Strewn over the parlor floor,
And the joys I knew in a far-off day
  Will gladden my heart once more.

Whoever has lived in a toy-strewn home,
  Though feeble he be and gray,
Will yearn, no matter how far he roam,
  For the glorious disarray
Of the little home with its littered floor
  That was his in the by-gone days;
And his heart will throb as it throbbed before,
  When he rests where a baby plays.

## Last Night the Baby Cried

Last night the baby cried.  And I,
   Roused from a sound and soothing sleep,
Wondered to hear that little cry.
   For ten long years in slumber deep
I've lived my nights, and so it seemed
That what I'd heard I'd only dreamed.

For ten long years a banging gate,
   The milkman's whistle, or the horn
Of motors driven at rapid rate,
   Have wakened me at early dawn;
But late last night awake was I,
Thinking I'd heard a baby cry.

I leaned upon my elbow there
   And wondered did I dream or not?
But once again upon the air
   The call came from her tiny cot!
Then peacefully I turned and smiled
To hear the crying of our child.

Lonely and still the house has seemed
   For ten long years, but once again
We have the joy of which we'd dreamed —
   The joy which many seek in vain!
Oh, happy, happy home, thought I,
That wakes to hear a baby cry.

## Little Fishermen

A little ship goes out to sea
As soon as we have finished tea;
Off yonder where the big moon glows
This tiny little vessel goes,
But never grown-up eyes have seen
The ports to which this ship has been;
Upon the shore the old folks stand
Till morning brings it back to land.

In search of smiles this little ship
Each evening starts upon a trip;
Just smiles enough to last the day
Is it allowed to bring away;
So nightly to some golden shore
It must set out alone for more,
And sail the rippling sea for miles
Until the hold is full of smiles.

By gentle hands the sails are spread;
The stars are glistening overhead
And in that hour when tiny ships
Prepare to make their evening trips
The sea becomes a wondrous place,
As beautiful as mother's face;
And all the day's disturbing cries
Give way to soothing lullabies.

No clang of bell or warning shout
Is heard on shore when they put out;
The little vessels slip away
As silently as does the day.
And all night long on sands of gold
They cast their nets, and fill the hold
With smiles and joys beyond compare,
To cheer a world that's sad with care.


## The Cookie-Lady

She is gentle, kind and fair,
And there's silver in her hair;
She has known the touch of sorrow,
But the smile of her is sweet;
And sometimes it seems to me
That her mission is to be
The gracious cookie-lady
To the youngsters of the street.

All the children in the block
Daily stand beside the crock,
Where she keeps the sugar cookies
That the little folks enjoy;
And no morning passes o'er
That a tapping at her door

Doesn't warn her of the visit
Of a certain little boy.

She has made him feel that he
Has a natural right to be
In her kitchen when she's baking
Pies and cakes and ginger bread;
And each night to me he brings
All the pretty, tender things
About little by-gone children
That the cookie-lady said.

Oh, dear cookie-lady sweet,
May you beautify our street
With your kind and gentle presence
Many more glad years, I pray;
May the skies be bright above you,
As you've taught our babes to love you;
You will scar their hearts with sorrow
If you ever go away.

Life is strange, and when I scan it,
I believe God tries to plan it,
So that where He sends his babies
In that neighborhood to dwell,
One of rare and gracious beauty
Shall abide, whose sweetest duty
Is to be the cookie-lady
That the children love so well.

## Being Brave at Night

The other night 'bout two o'clock, or maybe it
    was three,
An elephant with shining tusks came chasing
    after me.
His trunk was wavin' in the air an' spoutin' jets
    of steam
An' he was out to eat me up, but still I didn't
    scream
Or let him see that I was scared — a better
    thought I had,
I just escaped from where I was an' crawled
    in bed with dad.

One time there was a giant who was horrible
    to see,
He had three heads an' twenty arms, an' he
    come after me
An' red hot fire came from his mouths an'
    every hand was red
An' he declared he'd grind my bones an' make
    them into bread.
But I was just too smart for him, I fooled him
    mighty bad,
Before his hands could collar me I crawled in
    bed with dad.

I ain't scared of nothing that comes pesterin'
me at night.
Once I was chased by forty ghosts all shimmery
an' white,
An' I just raced 'em round the room an' let 'em
think maybe
I'd have to stop an' rest awhile, when they could
capture me.
Then when they leapt onto my bed, Oh Gee!
but they were mad
To find that I had slipped away an' crawled in
bed with dad.

No giants, ghosts or elephants have dared to
come in there
'Coz if they did he'd beat 'em up and chase 'em
to their lair.
They just hang 'round the children's rooms an'
snap an' snarl an' bite
An' laugh if they can make 'em yell for help
with all their might,
But I don't ever yell out loud.  I'm not that sort
of lad,
I slip from out the covers an' I crawl in bed
with dad.

## Pleasure's Signs

There's a bump on his brow and a smear on his
    cheek
  That is plainly the stain of his tears;
At his neck there's a glorious sun-painted streak,
  The bronze of his happiest years.
Oh, he's battered and bruised at the end of the
    day,
  But smiling before me he stands,
And somehow I like to behold him that way.
  Yes, I like him with dirt on his hands.

Last evening he painfully limped up to me
  His tale of adventure to tell;
He showed me a grime-covered cut on his knee,
  And told me the place where he fell.
His clothing was stained to the color of clay,
  And he looked to be nobody's lad,
But somehow I liked to behold him that way,
  For it spoke of the fun that he'd had.

Let women-folk prate as they will of a boy
  Who is heedless of knickers and shirt;
I hold that the badge of a young fellow's joy
  Are cheeks that are covered with dirt.
So I look for him nightly to greet me that way,
  His joys and misfortunes to tell,
For I know by the signs that he wears of his play
  That the lad I'm so fond of is well.

God made the little boys for fun, for rough and
    tumble times of play;
He made their little legs to run and race and
    scamper through the day.
He made them strong for climbing trees, he
    suited them for horns and drums,
And filled them full of revelries so they could be
    their father's chums.
But then He saw that gentle ways must also
    travel from above.
And so, through all our troubled days He sent
    us little girls to love.

He knew that earth would never do, unless a bit
    of Heaven it had.
Men needed eyes divinely blue to toil by day and
    still be glad.
A world where only men and boys made merry
    would in time grow stale,
And so He shared His Heavenly joys that faith
    in Him should never fail.
He sent us down a thousand charms, He decked
    our ways with golden curls
And laughing eyes and dimpled arms. He let us
    have His little girls.

They are the tenderest of His flowers, the little
  angels of His flock,
And we may keep and call them ours, until God's
  messenger shall knock.
They bring to us the gentleness and beauty that
  we sorely need;
They soothe us with each fond caress and
  strengthen us for every deed.
And happy should that mortal be whom God has
  trusted, through the years,
To guard a little girl and see that she is kept
  from pain and tears.


## Dinner-Time

Tuggin' at your bottle,
  An' it's O, you're mighty sweet!
Just a bunch of dimples
  From your top-knot to your feet,
Lyin' there an' gooin'
  In the happiest sort o' way,
Like a rosebud peekin' at me
  In the early hours o' day;
Gloatin' over goodness
  That you know an' sense an' clutch,

An' smilin' at your daddy,
  Who loves you, O, so much!

Tuggin' at your bottle,
  As you nestle in your crib,
With your daddy grinnin' at you
  'Cause you've dribbled on your bib,
An' you gurgle an' you chortle
  Like a brook in early Spring;
An' you kick your pink feet gayly,
  An' I think you'd like to sing.
All you wanted was your dinner,
  Daddy knew it too, you bet!
An' the moment that you got it
  Then you ceased to fuss an' fret.

Tuggin' at your bottle,
  Not a care, excepting when
You lose the rubber nipple,
  But you find it soon again;
An' the gurglin' an' the gooin'
  An' the chortlin' start anew,
An' the kickin' an' the squirmin'
  Show the wondrous joy o' you.
But I'll bet you're not as happy
  At your dinner, little tot,
As the weather-beaten daddy
  Who is bendin' o'er your cot!

# Castor Oil

I don't mind lickin's, now an' then,
An' I can even stand it when
My mother calls me in from play
To run some errand right away.
There's things 'bout bein' just a boy
That ain't all happiness an' joy,
But I suppose I've got to stand
My share o' trouble in this land,
An' I ain't kickin' much — but, say,
The worst of parents is that they
Don't realize just how they spoil
A feller's life with castor oil.

Of all the awful stuff, Gee Whiz!
That is the very worst there is.
An' every time if I complain,
Or say I've got a little pain,
There's nothing else that they can think
'Cept castor oil for me to drink.
I notice, though, when Pa is ill,
That he gets fixed up with a pill,
An' Pa don't handle Mother rough
An' make her swallow nasty stuff;
But when I've got a little ache,
It's castor oil I've got to take.

I don't mind goin' up to bed
Afore I get the chapter read;
I don't mind bein' scolded, too,
For lots of things I didn't do;
But, Gee! I hate it when they say,
"Come! Swallow this — an' right away!"
Let poets sing about the joy
It is to be a little boy,
I'll tell the truth about my case:
The poets here can have my place,
An' I will take their life of toil
If they will take my castor oil.


## At Dawn

They come to my room at the break of the day,
With their faces all smiles and their minds full
    of play;
They come on their tip-toes and silently creep
To the edge of the bed where I'm lying asleep,
And then at a signal, on which they agree,
With a shout of delight they jump right onto me.
They lift up my eyelids and tickle my nose,
And scratch at my cheeks with their little pink
    toes;

And sometimes to give them a laugh and a scare
I snap and I growl like a cinnamon bear;
Then over I roll, and with three kids astride
I gallop away on their feather-bed ride.

I've thought it all over.  Man's biggest mistake
Is in wanting to sleep when his babes are awake;
When they come to his room for that first bit of
     fun
He should make up his mind that his sleeping is
     done;
He should share in the laughter they bring to
     his side
And start off the day with that feather-bed ride.

Oh, they're fun at their breakfast and fun at
     their lunch;
Any hour of the day they're a glorious bunch!
When they're togged up for Sundays they're
     certainly fine,
And I'm glad in my heart I can call them all
     mine,
But I think that the time that I like them the best
Is that hour in the morning before they are
     dressed.

## Bud Discusses Cleanliness

First thing in the morning, last I hear at night,
Get it when I come from school: "My, you
    look a sight!
Go upstairs this minute, an' roll your sleeves
    up high
An' give your hands a scrubbing an' wipe 'em
    till they're dry!
Now don't stand there and argue, an' never
    mind your tears!
An' this time please remember to wash your
    neck and ears."

Can't see why ears grow on us, all crinkled
    like a shell,
With lots of fancy carvings that make a feller
    yell
Each time his Ma digs in them to get a speck
    of dirt,
When plain ones would be easy to wash an'
    wouldn't hurt.
An' I can't see the reason why every time Ma
    nears,
She thinks she's got to send me to wash my
    neck an' ears.

I never wash to suit her; don't think I ever will.
If I was white as sister, she'd call me dirty still.
At night I get a scrubbing an' go to bed, an'
then
The first thing in the morning, she makes me
wash again.
That strikes me as ridiklus; I've thought of it
a heap.
A feller can't get dirty when he is fast asleep.

When I grow up to be a man like Pa, an' have
a wife
An' kids to boss around, you bet they'll have an
easy life.
We won't be at them all the time, the way they
keep at me,
An' kick about a little dirt that no one else can
see.
An' every night at supper time as soon as he
appears,
We will not chase our boy away to wash his
neck an' ears.

# The Children

The children bring us laughter, and the children
    bring us tears;
They string our joys, like jewels bright, upon
    the thread of years;
They bring the bitterest cares we know, their
    mothers' sharpest pain,
Then smile our world to loveliness, like sunshine
    after rain.

The children make us what we are; the childless
    king is spurned;
The children send us to the hills where glories
    may be earned;
For them we pledge our lives to strife, for them
    do mothers fade,
And count in new-born loveliness their sacrifice
    repaid.

The children bring us back to God; in eyes that
    dance and shine
Men read from day to day the proof of love and
    power divine;
For them are fathers brave and good and mothers
    fair and true,
For them is every cherished dream and every
    deed we do.

For children are the furnace fires of life kept
    blazing high;
For children on the battle fields are soldiers
    pleased to die;
In every place where humans toil, in every dream
    and plan,
The laughter of the children shapes the destiny
    of man.

## *His Example*

There are little eyes upon you, and they're watch-
    ing night and day;
There are little ears that quickly take in every
    word you say;
There are little hands all eager to do everything
    you do,
And a little boy is dreaming of the day he'll
    be like you.

You're the little fellow's idol, you're the wisest
    of the wise;
In his little mind about you no suspicions ever
    rise;

He believes in you devoutly, holds that all you
    say and do
He will say and do in your way when he's grown
    up just like you.

Oh, it sometimes makes me shudder when I hear
    my boy repeat
Some careless phrase I've uttered in the language
    of the street;
And it sets my heart to grieving when some little
    fault I see
And I know beyond all doubting that he picked
    it up from me.

There's a wide-eyed little fellow who believes
    you're always right,
And his ears are always open and he watches
    day and night;
You are setting an example every day in all
    you do
For the little boy who's waiting to grow up to
    be like you.

## The Fun of Forgiving

Sometimes I'm almost glad to hear when I get
    home that they've been bad;
And though I try to look severe, within my heart
    I'm really glad
When mother sadly tells to me the list of awful
    things they've done,
Because when they come tearfully, forgiving
    them is so much fun.

I like to have them all alone, with no one near
    to hear or see,
Then as their little faults they own, I like to take
    them on my knee
And talk it over and pretend the whipping soon
    must be begun;
And then to kiss them at the end — forgiving
    them is so much fun.

Within the world there's no such charm as chil-
    dren penitent and sad,
Who put two soft and chubby arms around your
    neck, when they've been bad.
And as you view their trembling lips, away your
    temper starts to run,
And from your mind all anger slips — forgiving
    them is so much fun.

If there were nothing to forgive I wonder if
    we'd love them so;
If they were wise enough to live as grown-ups
    do, and always go
Along the pleasant path of right, with ne'er a
    fault from sun to sun,
A lot of joys we'd miss at night — forgiving
    them is so much fun.


## The Right Family

With time our notions allus change,
An' years make old idees seem strange —
Take Mary there — time was when she
Thought one child made a family,
An' when our eldest, Jim, was born,
She used to say, both night an' morn':
" One little one to love an' keep,
To guard awake, an' watch asleep;
To bring up right an' lead him through
Life's path is all we ought to do."

Two years from then our Jennie came,
But Mary didn't talk the same;
" Now that's just right," she said to me,
" We've got the proper family —

A boy an' girl, God sure is good;
It seems as though He understood
That I've been hopin' every way
To have a little girl some day;
Sometimes I've prayed the whole night
    through —
One ain't enough; we needed two."

Then as the months went rollin' on,
One day the stork brought little John,
An' Mary smiled an' said to me;
"The proper family is three;
Two boys, a girl to romp an' play —
Jus' work enough to fill the day.
I never had enough to do,
The months that we had only two;
Three's jus' right, pa, we don't want more."
Still time went on an' we had four.

An' that was years ago, I vow,
An' we have six fine children now;
An' Mary's plumb forgot the day
She used to sit an' sweetly say
That one child was enough for her
To love an' give the proper care;
One, two or three or four or five —
Why, goodness gracious, sakes alive,
If God should send her ten to-night,
She'd vow her fam'ly was jus' right!

95

# Tonsils

One day the doctor came because my throat was
    feeling awful sore,
An' when he looked inside to see he said: "It's
    like it was before;
It's tonserlitis, sure enough.  You'd better tell
    her Pa to-day
To make his mind up now to have that little
    party right away."

I'd heard him talk that way before when Bud
    was sick, an' so I knew
That what they did to him that time, to me they
    planned to come an' do.
An' when my Pa came home that night Ma said:
    " She can't grow strong an' stout
Until the doctor comes an' takes her addynoids
    an' tonsils out."

An' then Pa took me on his knee an' kissed me
    solemn-like an' grave,
An' said he guessed it was the best, an' then he
    asked me to be brave.
Ma said: "Don't look at her like that, it's
    nothing to be scared about ";
An' Pa said: "True, but still I wish she needn't
    have her tonsils out."

Next morning when I woke, Ma said I couldn't
    have my breakfast then,
Because the doctors an' the nurse had said they
    would be here by ten.
When they got here the doctor smiled an' gave
    me some perfume to smell,
An' told me not to cry at all, coz pretty soon
    I would be well.

When I woke up Ma smiled an' said: "It's all
    right now"; but in my head
It seemed like wheels were buzzing round an'
    everywhere I looked was red.
An' I can't eat hard cookies yet, nor use my
    voice at all to shout,
But Pa an' Ma seem awful glad that I have had
    my tonsils out.

## As It Goes

In the corner she's left the mechanical toy,
  On the chair is her Teddy Bear fine;
The things that I thought she would really enjoy
  Don't seem to be quite in her line.
There's the flaxen-haired doll that is lovely to see
  And really expensively dressed,
Left alone, all uncared for, and strange though
      it be,
  She likes her rag dolly the best.


Oh, the money we spent and the plans that we
      laid
  And the wonderful things that we bought!
There are toys that are cunningly, skillfully
      made,
  But she seems not to give them a thought.
She was pleased when she woke and discovered
      them there,
  But never a one of us guessed
That it isn't the splendor that makes a gift
      rare —
  She likes her rag dolly the best.

There's the flaxen-haired doll, with the real
    human hair,
  There's the Teddy Bear left all alone,
There's the automobile at the foot of the stair,
  And there is her toy telephone;
We thought they were fine, but a little child's
    eyes
  Look deeper than ours to find charm,
And now she's in bed, and the rag dolly lies
  Snuggled close on her little white arm.


## When the Soap Gets in Your Eye

My father says that I ought to be
A man when anything happens to me.
An' he says that a man will take a blow
An' never let on it hurts him so;
He'll grit his teeth an' he'll set his chin
An' bear his pain with a manly grin.
But I'll bet that the bravest man would cry
If ever the soap gets into his eye.
I'm brave enough when I'm playin' ball,
An' I can laugh when I've had a fall.

With the girls around I'd never show
That I was scared if the blood should flow
From my banged up nose or a battered knee.
As brave as the bravest I can be,
But it's different pain, an' I don't know why,
Whenever the soap gets into your eye.

I can set my teeth an' I can grin
When I scrape my cheek or I bark my shin,
An' once I fell from our apple tree
An' the wind was knocked right out of me,
But I never cried an' the gang all said
That they thought for sure I was really dead.
But it's worse than thinking you're going to die
Whenever the soap gets into your eye.

When your mother's holding your neck, and you
Couldn't get away if you wanted to,
An' she's latherin' hard with her good right hand,
It's more than the bravest man could stand.
If you open your mouth to howl, you get
A taste of the wash rag, cold and wet,
But you got to yell till your face gets dry
Whenever the soap gets into your eye.

# I Don't Want to Go to Bed

World wide over this is said:
" I don't want to go to bed."
Dads and mothers, far and near,
Every night this chorus hear;
Makes no difference where they are,
Here or off in Zanzibar,
In the igloos made of snow
Of the fur-clad Eskimo,
In the blistering torrid zone,
This one touch of nature's known;
In life's various tongues it's said:
" I don't want to go to bed!"

This has ever been the way
Of the youngsters at their play.
Laughter quickly dries their tears,
Trouble swiftly disappears,
Joy is everywhere about,
Here and there and in and out;
Yet when night comes on they cry
That so glad a day should die,
And they think that they will miss
Something more of precious bliss,
So shouts every curly-head:
" I don't want to go to bed!"

Age is glad to put away
All the burdens of the day,

Glad to lay the worries down,
Quit the noises of the town,
And in slumber end the care
That has met them here and there.
But the children do not know
Life is freighted down with woe;
They would run until they drop,
Hoping day would never stop,
Calling back when it has fled:
" I don't want to go to bed."


## Morning Brigands

There may be happier times than this,
  But if there are I've never known them,
When youngsters jump in bed to kiss
  And wake the pa's and ma's who own them.
What if the sun be up or not,
  Another perfect day is dawning,
And is it not a happy lot
  With such delight to greet the morning?

Sometimes I hear them quit their bed
  And catch their bare-foot pitter-patter,

And other times they're at my head
  Before I know what is the matter.
Brigands to rob us of our sleep
  They come — their weapons love and laughter,
And though we're locked in slumber deep,
  They always get the joy they're after.

Some days there are when we would lie
  And dream our dreams a little longer,
Then " back to bed awhile," we cry —
  But oh, our love for them is stronger,
Yes, stronger than our wish to sleep,
  And so we countermand the order
And let that pair of brigands leap
  With wild delight across love's border.

There may be happier times than this,
  But if there are I've never known them,
When youngsters jump in bed to kiss
  And wake the pa's and ma's who own them.
They miss a lot, the man and wife
  Who never feel those glad hands shake them,
Who rise by day to toil and strife,
  But have no little tots to wake them.

## Aunty

I'm sorry for a feller if he hasn't any aunt,
To let him eat an' do the things his mother says
    he can't.
An aunt to come a visitin' or one to go an' see
Is just about the finest kind of lady there could be.
Of course she's not your mother, an' she hasn't
    got her ways,
But a part that's most important in a feller's life
    she plays.

She is kind an' she is gentle, an' sometimes she's
    full of fun,
An' she's very sympathetic when some dreadful
    thing you've done.
An' she likes to buy you candy, an' she's always
    gettin' toys
That you wish your Pa would get you, for she
    hasn't any boys.
But sometimes she's over-loving, an' your cheeks
    turn red with shame
When she smothers you with kisses, but you like
    her just the same.

One time my father took me to my aunty's, an'
    he said:
" You will stay here till I get you, an' be sure
    you go to bed
When your aunty says it's time to, an' be good
    an' mind her, too,
An' when you come home we'll try to have a big
    surprise for you."
I did as I was told to, an' when Pa came back
    for me
He said there was a baby at the house for me
    to see.

I've been visitin' at aunty's for a week or two,
    an' Pa
Has written that he's comin' soon to take me
    home to Ma.
He says they're gettin' lonely, an' I'm kind o'
    lonely, too,
Coz an aunt is not exactly what your mother is
    to you.
I am hungry now to see her, but I'm wondering
    to-day
If Pa's bought another baby in the time I've
    been away.

## Different

The kids at our house number three,
As different as they can be;
And if perchance they numbered six
Each one would have particular tricks,
And certain little whims and fads
Unlike the other girls and lads.
No two glad rascals can you name
Whom God has fashioned just the same.

Bud's tough and full of life and fun
And likes to race about and run,
And tease the girls; the rascal knows
The slyest ways to pinch a nose,
And yank a curl until it hurts,
And disarrange their Sunday skirts.
Sometimes he trips them, heads o'er heels,
To glory in their frenzied squeals.

And Marjorie: She'd have more joy,
She thinks, if she'd been born a boy;
She wants no ribbons on her hair,
No fancy, fussy things to wear,

Things in which Sylvia delights
To Marjorie are dreadful frights.
They're sisters, yet I'd swear the name
Is all they own that is the same.

Proud Sylvia, beautiful to see,
A high-toned lady wants to be;
She'll primp and fuss and deck her hair
And gorgeous raiment wants to wear;
She'll sit sedately by the light
And read a fairy tale at night;
And she will sigh and sometimes wince
At all the trials of the prince.

If God should send us children nine
To follow our ancestral line,
I'd vow that in the lot we'd strike
No two among them just alike.
And that's the way it ought to be;
The larger grows the family,
The more we own of joy and bliss,
For each brings charms the others miss.

# A Fine Sight

I reckon the finest sight of all
  That a man can see in this world of ours
Ain't the works of art on the gallery wall,
  Or the red an' white o' the fust spring flowers,
Or a hoard o' gold from the yellow mines;
  But the sight that'll make ye want t' yell
Is t' catch a glimpse o' the fust pink signs
  In yer baby's cheek, that she's gittin' well.

When ye see the pink jes' a-creepin' back
  T' the pale, drawn cheek, an' ye note a smile,
Then th' cords o' yer heart that were tight, grow
      slack
  An' ye jump fer joy every little while,
An' ye tiptoe back to her little bed
  As though ye doubted yer eyes, or were
Afraid it was fever come back instead,
  An' ye found that th' pink still blossomed
      there.

Ye've watched fer that smile an' that bit o' bloom
  With a heavy heart fer weeks an' weeks;
An' a castle o' joy becomes that room
  When ye glimpse th' pink in yer baby's cheeks.
An' out o' yer breast flies a weight o' care,
  An' ye're lifted up by some magic spell,
An' yer heart jes' naturally beats a prayer
  O' joy to the Lord 'cause she's gittin' well.

# A Boy at Christmas

If I could have my wish to-night it would not be
    for wealth or fame,
It would not be for some delight that men who
    live in luxury claim,
But it would be that I might rise at three or four
    a. m. to see,
With eager, happy, boyish eyes, my presents on
    the Christmas tree.
Throughout this world there is no joy, I know
    now I am growing gray,
So rich as being just a boy, a little boy on Christ-
    mas Day.

I'd like once more to stand and gaze enraptured
    on a tinseled tree,
With eyes that know just how to blaze, a heart
    still tuned to ecstasy;
I'd like to feel the old delight, the surging thrills
    within me come;
To love a thing with all my might, to grasp the
    pleasure of a drum;
To know the meaning of a toy — a meaning lost
    to minds blasé;
To be just once again a boy, a little boy on
    Christmas Day.

I'd like to see a pair of skates the way they looked
    to me back then,
Before I'd turned from boyhood's gates and
    marched into the world of men;
I'd like to see a jackknife, too, with those same
    eager, dancing eyes
That couldn't fault or blemish view; I'd like to
    feel the same surprise,
The pleasure, free from all alloy, that has forever
    passed away,
When I was just a little boy and had my faith in
    Christmas Day.

Oh, little, laughing, roguish lad, the king that
    rules across the sea
Would give his scepter if he had such joy as now
    belongs to thee!
And beards of gray would give their gold, and
    all the honors they possess,
Once more within their grasp to hold thy present
    fee of happiness.
Earth sends no greater, surer joy, as, too soon,
    thou, as I, shall say,
Than that of him who is a boy, a little boy on
    Christmas Day.

# *The Cut-Down Trousers*

When father couldn't wear them mother cut them
  down for me;
She took the slack in fore and aft, and hemmed
  them at the knee;
They fitted rather loosely, but the things that
  made me glad
Were the horizontal pockets that those good old
  trousers had.

They shone like patent leather just where well-
  worn breeches do,
But the cloth in certain portions was considered
  good as new,
And I know that I was envied by full many a
  richer lad
For the horizontal pockets that those good old
  knickers had.

They were cut along the waist line, with the open-
  ing straight and wide,
And there wasn't any limit to what you could get
  inside;
They would hold a peck of marbles, and a knife
  and top and string,
And snakes and frogs and turtles; there was
  room for everything.

Then our fortune changed a little, and my mother
    said that she
Wouldn't bother any longer fitting father's duds
    on me,
But the store clothes didn't please me; there were
    times they made me sad,
For I missed those good old pockets that my
    father's trousers had.


## *The Little Hurts*

Every night she runs to me
With a bandaged arm or a bandaged knee,
A stone-bruised heel or a swollen brow,
And in sorrowful tones she tells me how
She fell and "hurted herse'f to-day"
While she was having the "bestest play."

And I take her up in my arms and kiss
The new little wounds and whisper this:
"Oh, you must be careful, my little one,
You musn't get hurt while your daddy's gone,
For every cut with its ache and smart
Leaves another bruise on your daddy's heart."

Every night I must stoop to see
The fresh little cuts on her arm or knee;
The little hurts that have marred her play,
And brought the tears on a happy day;
For the path of childhood is oft beset
With care and trouble and things that fret.

Oh, little girl, when you older grow,
Far greater hurts than these you'll know;
Greater bruises will bring your tears,
Around the bend of the lane of years,
But come to your daddy with them at night
And he'll do his best to make all things right.


## Grown Up

Last year he wanted building blocks,
    And picture books and toys,
A saddle horse that gayly rocks,
    And games for little boys.
But now he's big and all that stuff
    His whim no longer suits;
He tells us that he's old enough
    To ask for rubber boots.

Last year whatever Santa brought
    Delighted him to own;
He never gave his wants a thought
    Nor made his wishes known.
But now he says he wants a gun,
    The kind that really shoots,
And I'm confronted with a son
    Demanding rubber boots.

The baby that we used to know
    Has somehow slipped away,
And when or where he chanced to go
    Not one of us can say.
But here's a helter-skelter lad
    That to me nightly scoots
And boldly wishes that he had
    A pair of rubber boots.

I'll bet old Santa Claus will sigh
    When down our flue he comes,
And seeks the babe that used to lie
    And suck his tiny thumbs,
And finds within that little bed
    A grown up boy who hoots
At building blocks, and wants instead
    A pair of rubber boots.

## Grandpa

My grandpa is the finest man
Excep' my pa.  My grandpa can
Make kites and carts and lots of things
You pull along the ground with strings,
And he knows all the names of birds,
And how they call 'thout using words,
And where they live and what they eat,
And how they build their nests so neat.
He's lots of fun!  Sometimes all day
He comes to visit me and play.
You see he's getting old, and so
To work he doesn't have to go,
And when it isn't raining, he
Drops in to have some fun with me.

He takes my hand and we go out
And everything we talk about.
He tells me how God makes the trees,
And why it hurts to pick up bees.
Sometimes he stops and shows to me
The place where fairies used to be;
And then he tells me stories, too,
And I am sorry when he's through.
When I am asking him for more

He says: "Why, there's a candy store!
Let's us go there and see if they
Have got the kind we like to-day."
Then when we get back home my ma
Says: "You are spoiling Buddy, Pa."

My grandpa is my mother's pa,
I guess that's what all grandpas are.
And sometimes ma, all smiles, will say:
"You didn't always act that way.
When I was little, then you said
That children should be sent to bed
And not allowed to rule the place
And lead old folks a merry chase."
And grandpa laughs and says: "That's **true**,
That's what I used to say to you.
It is a father's place to show
The young the way that they should go,
But grandpas have a different task,
Which is to get them all they ask."

## Pa Did It

The train of cars that Santa brought is out of
    kilter now;
While pa was showing how they went he broke
    the spring somehow.
They used to run around a track — at least they
    did when he
Would let me take them in my hands an' wind
    'em with a key.
I could 'a' had some fun with 'em, if only they
    would go,
But, gee! I never had a chance, for pa enjoyed
    'em so.

The automobile that I got that ran around the
    floor
Was lots of fun when it was new, but it won't
    go no more.
Pa wound it up for Uncle Jim to show him how
    it went,
An' when those two got through with it the
    runnin' gear was bent,
An' now it doesn't go at all.  I mustn't grumble
    though,
'Cause while it was in shape to run my pa enjoyed
    it so.

I've got my blocks as good as new, my mitts **are**
　　perfect yet;
Although the snow is on the ground I haven't
　　got 'em wet.
I've taken care of everything that Santa brought
　　to me,
Except the toys that run about when wound up
　　with a key.
But next year you can bet I won't make any such
　　mistake;
I'm going to ask for toys an' things that **my pa**
　　cannot break.

## The Doctor

I don't see why Pa likes him so,
　　And seems so glad to have him come;
He jabs my ribs and wants to know
　　If here and there it's hurting some.
He holds my wrist, 'coz there are things
　　In there, which always jump and jerk,
Then, with a telephone he brings,
　　He listens to my breather work.
He taps my back and pinches me,
　　Then hangs a mirror on his head

And looks into my throat to see
  What makes it hurt and if it's red.
Then on his knee he starts to write
  And says to mother, with a smile:
" This ought to fix him up all right,
  We'll cure him in a little while."

I don't see why Pa likes him so.
  Whenever I don't want to play
He says: " The boy is sick, I know!
  Let's get the doctor right away."
And when he comes, he shakes his hand,
  And hustles him upstairs to me,
And seems contented just to stand
  Inside the room where he can see.

Then Pa says every time he goes:
  " That's money I am glad to pay;
It's worth it, when a fellow knows
  His pal will soon be up to play."
But maybe if my Pa were me,
  And had to take his pills and all,
He wouldn't be so glad to see
  The doctor come to make a call.

# The Little Velvet Suit

Last night I got to thinkin' of the pleasant long
    ago,
When I still had on knee breeches, an' I wore
    a flowing bow,
An' my Sunday suit was velvet.  Ma an' Pa
    thought it was fine,
But I know I didn't like it — either velvet or
    design;
It was far too girlish for me, for I wanted some-
    thing rough
Like what other boys were wearing, but Ma
    wouldn't buy such stuff.

Ma answered all my protests in her sweet an'
    kindly way;
She said it didn't matter what I wore to run an'
    play,
But on Sundays when all people went to church
    an' wore their best,
Her boy must look as stylish an' as well kept as
    the rest.
So she dressed me up in velvet, an' she tied the
    flowing bow,
An' she straightened out my stockings, so that
    not a crease would show.

An' then I chuckled softly to myself while dream-
	ing there
An' I saw her standing o'er me combing out my
	tangled hair.
I could feel again the tugging, an' I heard the
	yell I gave
When she struck a snarl, an' softly I could hear
	her say: " Be brave.
'Twill be over in a minute, and a little man like
	you
Shouldn't whimper at a little bit of pain the way
	you do."

Oh, I wouldn't mind the tugging at my scalp
	lock, and I know
That I'd gladly wear to please her that old flow-
	ing girlish bow;
And I think I'd even try to don once more that
	velvet suit,
And blush the same old blushes, as the women
	called me cute,
Could the dear old mother only take me by the
	hand again,
And be as proud of me right now as she was
	always then.

# Spoiling Them

"You're spoiling them!" the mother cries
When I give way to weepy eyes
And let them do the things they wish,
Like cleaning up the jelly dish,
Or finishing the chocolate cake,
Or maybe let the rascal take
My piece of huckleberry pie,
Because he wants it more than I.

"You're spoiling them!" the mother tells,
When I am heedless to their yells,
And let them race and romp about
And do not put their joy to rout.
I know I should be firm, and yet
I tried it once to my regret;
I will remember till I'm old
The day I started in to scold.

I stamped my foot and shouted: "Stop!"
And Bud just let his drum sticks drop,
And looked at me, and turned away;
That night there was no further play.
The girls were solemn-like and still,
Just as girls are when they are ill,
And when unto his cot I crept,
I found him sobbing as he slept.

That was my first attempt and last
To play the scold.  I'm glad it passed
So quickly and has left no trace
Of memory on each little face;
But now when mother whispers low:
" You're spoiling them," I answer, " No!
But it is plain as plain can be,
Those little tykes are spoiling me."


## Story Time

" Tell us a story," comes the cry
    From little lips when nights are cold,
And in the grate the flames leap high.
    " Tell us a tale of pirates bold,
Or fairies hiding in the glen,
    Or of a ship that's wrecked at sea."
I fill my pipe, and there and then
    Gather the children round my knee.


I give them all a role to play —
    No longer are they youngsters small,
And I, their daddy, turning gray;
    We are adventurers, one and all.
We journey forth as Robin Hood
    In search of treasure, or to do

Some deed of daring or of good;
  Our hearts are ever brave and true.

We take a solemn oath to be
  Defenders of the starry flag;
We brave the winter's stormy sea,
  Or climb the rugged mountain crag,
To battle to the death with those
  Who would defame our native land;
We pitch our camp among the snows
  Or on the tropics' burning sand.

We rescue maidens, young and fair,
  Held captive long in prison towers;
We slay the villain in his lair,
  For we're possessed of magic powers.
And though we desperately fight,
  When by our foes are we beset,
We always triumph for the right;
  We have not lost a battle yet.

It matters not how far we stray,
  Nor where our battle lines may be,
We never get so far away
  That we must spend a night at sea.
It matters not how high we climb,
  How many foes our pathway block,
We always conquer just in time
  To go to bed at 9 o'clock.

## Another Mouth to Feed

We've got another mouth to feed,
   From out our little store;
To satisfy another's need
   Is now my daily chore.
A growing family is ours,
   Beyond the slightest doubt;
It takes all my financial powers
   To keep them looking stout.
With us another makes his bow
   To breakfast, dine and sup;
Our little circle's larger now,
   For Buddy's got a pup.

If I am frayed about the heels
   And both my elbows shine
And if my overcoat reveals
   The poverty that's mine,
'Tis not because I squander gold
   In folly's reckless way;
The cost of foodstuffs, be it told,
   Takes all my weekly pay.
'Tis putting food on empty plates
   That eats my wages up;
And now another mouth awaits,
   For Buddy's got a pup.

And yet I gladly stand the strain,
   And count the task worth while.

Nor will I dismally complain
    While Buddy wears a smile.
What's one mouth more at any board
    Though costly be the fare?
The poorest of us can afford
    His frugal meal to share.
And so bring on the extra plate,
    He will not need a cup,
And gladly will I pay the freight
    Now Buddy's got a pup.

## The Lure That Failed

I know a wonderful land, I said,
    Where the skies are always blue,
Where on chocolate drops are the children fed,
    And cocoanut cookies, too;
Where puppy dogs romp at the children's feet,
    And the liveliest kittens play,
And little tin soldiers guard the street
    To frighten the bears away.

This land is reached by a wonderful ship
    That sails on a golden tide;

But never a grown-up makes the trip —
  It is only a children's ride.
And never a cross-patch journeys there,
  And never a pouting face,
For it is the Land of Smiling, where
  A frown is a big disgrace.


Oh, you board the ship when the sun goes down,
  And over a gentle sea
You slip away from the noisy town
  To the land of the chocolate tree.
And there, till the sun comes over the hill,
  You frolic and romp and play,
And of candy and cake you eat your fill,
  With no one to tell you "Nay!"


So come! It is time for the ship to go
  To this wonderful land so fair,
And gently the summer breezes blow
  To carry you safely there.
So come! Set sail on this golden sea,
  To the land that is free from dread!
"I know what you mean," she said to me,
  "An' I don't wanna go to bed."

## The Little Army

Little women, little men,
Childhood never comes again.
Live it gayly while you may;
Give your baby souls to play;
   March to sound of stick and pan,
     In your paper hats, and tramp
   Just as bravely as you can
     To your pleasant little camp.
Wooden sword and wooden gun
Make a battle splendid fun.
Fine the victories you win:
Dimpled cheek and dimpled chin.

Little women, little men,
Hearts are light when years are ten;
Eyes are bright and cheeks are red
When life's cares lie all ahead.
   Drums make merry music when
     They are leading children out;
   Trumpet calls are cheerful then,
     Glorious is the battle shout.
Little soldiers, single file,
Uniformed in grin and smile,
Conquer every foe they meet
Up and down the gentle street.

Little women, little men,
Would that youth could come again!
Would that I might fall in line
As a little boy of nine,
　　But with broomstick for a gun,
　　　　And with paper hat that I
　　Bravely wore back there for fun,
　　　　Never more may I defy
Foes that deep in ambush kneel —
Now my warfare's grim and real.
I that once was brave and bold,
Now am battered, bruised and old.

Little women, little men,
Planning to attack my den,
Little do you know the joy
That you give a worn-out boy
　　As he hears your gentle feet
　　　　Pitter-patting in the hall;
　　Gladly does he wait to meet
　　　　Conquest by a troop so small.
Dimpled cheek and dimpled chin,
You have but to smile to win.
Come and take him where he stays
Dreaming of his by-gone days.

# The Broken Drum

There is sorrow in the household;
There's a grief too hard to bear;
There's a little cheek that's tear-stained;
There's a sobbing baby there.
And try how we will to comfort,
Still the tiny teardrops come;
For, to solve a vexing problem,
Curly Locks has wrecked his drum.

It had puzzled him and worried,
How the drum created sound,
For he couldn't understand it;
It was not enough to pound
With his tiny hands and drumsticks,
And at last the day has come,
When another hope is shattered;
Now in ruins lies his drum.

With his metal bank he broke it,
Tore the tightened skin aside,
Gazed on vacant space bewildered,
Then he broke right down and cried.
For the broken bubble shocked him
And the baby tears must come;
Now a joy has gone forever:
Curly Locks has wrecked his drum.

While his mother tries to soothe him,
I am sitting here alone;
In the life that lies behind me,
Many shocks like that I've known.
And the boy who's upstairs weeping,
In the years that are to come
Will learn that many pleasures
Are as empty as his drum.

## The Boy Soldier

Each evening on my lap there climbs
  A little boy of three,
And with his dimpled, chubby fists
  He pounds me shamefully.
He gives my beard a vicious tug,
  He bravely pulls my nose;
And then he tussles with my hair
  And then explores my clothes.

He throws my pencils on the floor;
  My watch is his delight;
He never seems to think that I
  Have any private right.

And though he breaks my good cigars,
  With all his cunning art,
He works a greater ruin, far,
  Deep down within my heart.

This roguish little tyke who sits
  Each night upon my knee,
And hammers at his poor old dad,
  Is bound to conquer me.
He little knows that long ago,
  He forced the gates apart,
And marched triumphantly into
  The city of my heart.

Some day perhaps, in years to come,
  When he is older grown,
He, too, will be assailed as I,
  By youngsters of his own.
And when at last a little lad
  Gives battle on his knee,
I know that he'll be captured, too,
  Just as he captured me.

# A Bear Story

There was a bear — his name was Jim,
An' children weren't askeered of him,
An' he lived in a cave, where he
Was comfortubbul as could be,
An' in that cave, so my Pa said,
Jim always kept a stock of bread
An' honey, so that he could treat
The boys an' girls along his street.

An' all that Jim could say was " Woof! "
An' give a grunt that went like " Soof! "
An' Pa says when his grunt went off
It sounded jus' like Grandpa's cough,
Or like our Jerry when he's mad
An' growls at peddler men that's bad.
While grown-ups were afraid of Jim,
Kids could do anything with him.

One day a little boy like me
That had a sister Marjorie,
Was walking through the woods, an' they
Heard something " woofing " down that way,
An' they was scared an' stood stock still
An' wished they had a gun to kill
Whatever 'twas, but little boys
Don't have no guns that make a noise.

An' soon the "woofing" closer grew,
An' then a bear came into view,

The biggest bear you ever saw —
Ma's muff was smaller than his paw.
He saw the children an' he said:
" I ain't a-goin' to kill you dead;
You needn't turn away an' run;
I'm only scarin' you for fun."

An' then he stood up just like those
Big bears in circuses an' shows,
An' danced a jig, an' rolled about
An' said " Woof! Woof!" which meant " Look
    out!"
An' turned a somersault as slick
As any boy can do the trick.
Those children had been told of Jim
An' they decided it was him.

They stroked his nose when they got brave,
An' followed him into his cave,
An' Jim asked them if they liked honey,
They said they did.  Said Jim:  " That's funny.
I've asked a thousand boys or so
That question, an' not one's said no."
What happened then I cannot say
'Cause next I knew 'twas light as day.

## When Pa Comes Home

When Pa comes home, I'm at the door,
An' then he grabs me off the floor
An' throws me up an' catches me
When I come down, an' then, says he:
"Well, how'd you get along to-day?
An' were you good, an' did you play,
An' keep right out of mamma's way?
An' how'd you get that awful bump
Above your eye?  My, what a lump!
An' who spilled jelly on your shirt?
An' where'd you ever find the dirt
That's on your hands?  And my!  Oh, my!
I guess those eyes have had a cry,
They look so red.  What was it, pray?
What has been happening here to-day?"

An' then he drops his coat an' hat
Upon a chair, an' says:  "What's that?
Who knocked that engine on its back
An' stepped upon that piece of track?"
An' then he takes me on his knee
An' says:  "What's this that now I see?
Whatever can the matter be?
Who strewed those toys upon the floor,
An' left those things behind the door?
Who upset all those parlor chairs
An' threw those blocks upon the stairs?

I guess a cyclone called to-day
While I was workin' far away.
Who was it worried mamma so?
It can't be anyone I know."

An' then I laugh an' say: "It's me!
Me did most ever'thing you see.
Me got this bump the time we tripped.
An' here is where the jelly slipped
Right off my bread upon my shirt,
An' when me tumbled down it hurt.
That's how me got all over dirt.
Me threw those building blocks downstairs,
An' me upset the parlor chairs,
'Coz when you're playin' train you've got
To move things 'round an awful lot."
An' then my Pa he kisses me
An' bounces me upon his knee
An' says: "Well, well, my little lad,
What glorious fun you must have had!"

# The Joy of a Dog

Ma says no, it's too much care
An' it will scatter germs an' hair,
An' it's a nuisance through and through,
An' barks when you don't want it to;
An' carries dirt from off the street,
An' tracks the carpets with its feet.
But it's a sign he's growin' up
When he is longin' for a pup.

Most every night he comes to me
An' climbs a-straddle of my knee
An' starts to fondle me an' pet,
Then asks me if I've found one yet.
An' ma says: " Now don't tell him yes;
You know they make an awful mess,"
An' starts their faults to catalogue.
But every boy should have a dog.

An' some night when he comes to me,
Deep in my pocket there will be
The pup he's hungry to possess
Or else I sadly miss my guess.
For I remember all the joy
A dog meant to a little boy
Who loved it in the long ago —
The joy that's now his right to know.

## Up to the Ceiling

Up to the ceiling
And down to the floor,
Hear him now squealing
And calling for more.
Laughing and shouting,
" Away up!" he cries.
Who could be doubting
The love in his eyes.
Heigho! my baby!
And heigho! my son!
Up to the ceiling
Is wonderful fun.

Bigger than daddy
And bigger than mother;
Only a laddie,
But bigger than brother.
Laughing and crowing
And squirming and wriggling,
Cheeks fairly glowing,
Now cooing and giggling!
Down to the cellar,
Then quick as a dart
Up to the ceiling
Brings joy to the heart.

Gone is the hurry,
The anguish and sting,

The heartache and worry
That business cares bring;
Gone is the hustle,
The clamor for gold,
The rush and the bustle
The day's affairs hold.
Peace comes to the battered
Old heart of his dad,
When "up to the ceiling"
He plays with his lad.

## Answering Him

"When shall I be a man?" he said,
As I was putting him to bed.
"How many years will have to be
Before Time makes a man of me?
And will I be a man when I
Am grown up big?" I heaved a sigh,
Because it called for careful thought
To give the answer that he sought.

And so I sat him on my knee,
And said to him: "A man you'll be
When you have learned that honor brings
More joy than all the crowns of kings;

That it is better to be true
To all who know and trust in you
Than all the gold of earth to gain
If winning it shall leave a stain.

" When you can fight for victory sweet,
Yet bravely swallow down defeat,
And cling to hope and keep the right,
Nor use deceit instead of might;
When you are kind and brave and clean,
And fair to all and never mean;
When there is good in all you plan,
That day, my boy, you'll be a man.

" Some of us learn this truth too late;
That years alone can't make us great;
That many who are three-score ten
Have fallen short of being men,
Because in selfishness they fought
And toiled without refining thought;
And whether wrong or whether right
They lived but for their own delight.

" When you have learned that you must hold
Your honor dearer far than gold;
That no ill-gotten wealth or fame
Can pay you for your tarnished name;
And when in all you say or do
Of others you're considerate, too,
Content to do the best you can
By such a creed, you'll be a man."

## The Bumps and Bruises Doctor

I'm the bumps and bruises doctor;
  I'm the expert that they seek
When their rough and tumble playing
  Leaves a scar on leg or cheek.
I'm the rapid, certain curer
  For the wounds of every fall;
I'm the pain eradicator;
  I can always heal them all.

Bumps on little people's foreheads
  I can quickly smooth away;
I take splinters out of fingers
  Without very much delay.
Little sorrows I can banish
  With the magic of my touch;
I can fix a bruise that's dreadful
  So it isn't hurting much.

I'm the bumps and bruises doctor,
  And I answer every call,
And my fee is very simple,
  Just a kiss, and that is all.
And I'm sitting here and wishing
  In the years that are to be,
When they face life's real troubles,
  That they'll bring them all to me.

# Real Swimming

I saw him in the distance, as the train went
    speeding by,
A shivery little fellow standing in the sun to dry,
And a little pile of clothing very near him I could
    see.
He was owner of a gladness that had once be-
    longed to me;
I have shivered as he shivered, I have dried the
    way he dried,
I've stood naked in God's sunshine with my gar-
    ments at my side;
And I thought as I beheld him, of the many
    weary men
Who would like to go in swimming as a little
    boy again.

I saw him scarce a moment, yet I knew his lips
    were blue
And I knew his teeth were chattering just as mine
    were wont to do;
And I knew his merry playmates in the pond
    were splashing still,
I could tell how much he envied all the boys that
    never chill;

And throughout that lonesome journey, I kept
    living o'er and o'er
The joys of going swimming when no bathing
    suits we wore;
I was with that little fellow, standing chattering
    in the sun,
I was sharing in his shivers and a partner of his
    fun.


Back to me there came the pictures that I never
    shall forget
When I dared not travel homewards if my shock
    of hair was wet,
When I did my brief undressing under fine and
    friendly trees
In the days before convention rigged us up in
    b. v. d's;
And I dived for stones and metal on the mill
    pond's muddy floor,
Then stood naked in the sunshine till my blood
    grew warm once more.
I was back again, a youngster, in those golden
    days of old,
When my teeth were wont to chatter and my lips
    were blue with cold.

## Always Saying "Don't!"

Folks are queer as they can be,
Always sayin' "don't" to me;
Don't do this an' don't do that.
Don't annoy or tease the cat,
Don't throw stones, or climb a tree,
Don't play in the road. Oh, Gee!
Seems like when I want to play
"Don't" is all that they can say.

If I start to have some fun,
Someone hollers, "Don't you run!"
If I want to go an' play
Mother says: "Don't go away."
Seems my life is filled clear through
With the things I mustn't do.
All the time I'm shouted at:
"No, no, Sonny, don't do that!"

Don't shout so an' make a noise,
Don't play with those naughty boys,
Don't eat candy, don't eat pie,
Don't you laugh and don't you cry,
Don't stand up and don't you fall,
Don't do anything at all.
Seems to me both night an' day
"Don't" is all that they can say.

When I'm older in my ways
An' have little boys to raise,
Bet I'll let 'em race an' run
An' not always spoil their fun;
I'll not tell 'em all along
Everything they like is wrong;
An' you bet your life I won't
All the time be sayin' " don't."

## No Children!

No children in the house to play —
It must be hard to live that way!
I wonder what the people do
When night comes on and the work is through,
With no glad little folks to shout,
No eager feet to race about,
No youthful tongues to chatter on
About the joy that's been and gone?
The house might be a castle fine,
But what a lonely place to dine!

No children in the house at all,
No fingermarks upon the wall,

No corner where the toys are piled —
Sure indication of a child.
No little lips to breathe the prayer
That God shall keep you in His care,
No glad caress and welcome sweet
When night returns you to your street;
No little lips a kiss to give —
Oh, what a lonely way to live!

No children in the house! I fear
We could not stand it half a year.
What would we talk about at night,
Plan for and work with all our might,
Hold common dreams about and find
True union of heart and mind,
If we two had no greater care
Than what we both should eat and wear?
We never knew love's brightest flame
Until the day the baby came.

And now we could not get along
Without their laughter and their song.
Joy is not bottled on a shelf,
It cannot feed upon itself;
And even love, if it shall wear,
Must find its happiness in care;
Dull we'd become of mind and speech
Had we no little ones to teach.
No children in the house to play!
Oh, we could never live that way!

## To a Little Girl

Oh, little girl with eyes of brown
And smiles that fairly light the town,
I wonder if you really know
Just why it is we love you so,
And why — with all the little girls
With shining eyes and tangled curls
That throng and dance this big world through —
Our hearts have room for only you.

Since other little girls are gay
And laugh and sing and romp in play,
And all are beautiful to see,
Why should you mean so much to me?
And why should Mother, day and night,
Make you her source of all delight,
And always find in your caress
Her greatest sum of happiness?

Oh, there's a reason good for this,
You laughing little bright-eyed miss!
In all this town, with all its girls
With shining eyes and sun-kissed curls,
If we should search it through and through
We'd find not one so fair as you;
And none, however fair of face,
Within our hearts could take your place.

For, one glad day not long ago,
God sent you down to us below,
And said that you were ours to keep,
To guard awake and watch asleep;
And ever since the day you came
No other child has seemed the same;
No other smiles are quite so fair
As those which happily you wear.

We seem to live from day to day
To hear the things you have to say;
And just because God gave us you,
We prize the little things you do.
Though God has filled this world with flowers,
We like you best because you're ours —
In you our greatest joys we know,
And that is why we love you so.

# A Feller's Hat

It's funny 'bout a feller's hat —
He can't remember where it's at,
Or where he took it off, or when,
The time he's wantin' it again.
He knows just where he leaves his shoes;
His sweater he won't often lose;
An' he can find his rubbers, but
He can't tell where his hat is put.

A feller's hat gets anywhere.
Sometimes he'll find it in a chair,
Or on the sideboard, or maybe
It's in the kitchen, just where he
Gave it a toss beside the sink
When he came in to get a drink,
An' then forgot — but anyhow
He never knows where it is now.

A feller's hat is never where
He thinks it is when he goes there;
It's never any use to look
For it upon a closet hook,
'Cause it is always in some place
It shouldn't be, to his disgrace,
An' he will find it, like as not,
Behind some radiator hot.

A feller's hat can get away
From him most any time of day,

So he can't ever find it when
He wants it to go out again;
It hides in corners dark an' grim
An' seems to want to bother him;
It disappears from sight somehow —
I wish I knew where mine is now.

## Practicing Time

Always whenever I want to play
I've got to practice an hour a day,
Get through breakfast and make my bed,
And Mother says: "Marjorie, run ahead!
There's a time for work and a time for fun,
So go and get your practicing done."
And Bud, he chuckles and says to me:
"Yes, do your practicing, Marjorie."
A brother's an awful tease, you know,
And he just says that 'cause I hate it so.

They leave me alone in the parlor there
To play the scales or "The Maiden's Prayer,"
And if I stop, Mother's bound to call,
"Marjorie dear, you're not playing at all!
Don't waste your time, but keep right on,

Or you'll have to stay when the hour is gone."
Or maybe the maid looks in at me
And says: "You're not playing, as I can see.
Just hustle along — I've got work to do
And I can't dust the room until you get through."

Then when I've run over the scales and things
Like "The Fairies' Dance," or "The Mountain
        Springs,"
And my fingers ache and my head is sore,
I find I must sit there a half hour more.
An hour is terribly long, I say,
When you've got to practice and want to play.
So slowly at times has the big hand dropped
That I was sure that the clock had stopped,
But Mother called down to me: "Don't forget —
A full hour, please.  It's not over yet."

Oh, when I get big and have children, too,
There's one thing that I will never do —
I won't have brothers to tease the girls
And make them mad when they pull their curls
And laugh at them when they've got to stay
And practice their music an hour a day;
I won't have a maid like the one we've got,
That likes to boss you around a lot;
And I won't have a clock that can go so slow
When it's practice time, 'cause I hate it so.

# When There's Company for Tea

When there's company for tea
Things go mighty hard with me;
Got to sit an' wait an' wait
Till the last guest's cleaned his plate,
An' I mustn't ask Ma what
Kind of pie it is she's got,
Mustn't crunch my napkin up
Or dip cookies in my cup.

When there's company for tea
Home don't seem like home to me;
Got to wash my ears an' neck
Till they do not show a speck;
Got to brush my hair an' then
Got to change my waist again,
Then walk slowly down stairs an'
Try to be a gentleman.

When there's company for tea
Ma spends hours instructing me
How to eat an' what to say,
An' I can't go out to play
When I've finished, but must stay
Till Ma whispers: " Now you may! "
Sittin' still is not much fun
When you've got your supper done.

When there's company for tea,
Then the servant waits on me
Last instead of first, an' I
Mustn't talk when she comes by;
If the boys outside should call,
I don't answer 'em at all;
You'd never know that it was me
When there's company for tea.

## The Good Little Boy

Once there was a boy who never
Tore his clothes, or hardly ever;
Never made his sister mad,
Never whipped fer bein' bad,
Never scolded by his Ma,
Never frowned at by his Pa,
Always fit fer folks to see,
Always good as good could be.

This good little boy from Heaven,
So I'm told, was only seven,
Yet he never shed real tears
When his mother scrubbed his ears,
An' at times when he was dressed
Fer a party, in his best,
He was careful of his shirt
Not to get it smeared with dirt.

Used to study late at night,
Learnin' how to read an' write;
When he played a baseball game,
Right away he always came
When his mother called him in.
An' he never made a din
But was quiet as a mouse
When they'd comp'ny in the house.

Liked to wash his hands an' face,
Liked to work around the place;
Never, when he'd tired of play,
Left his wagon in the way,
Or his bat an' ball around —
Put 'em where they could be found;
An' that good boy married Ma,
An' to-day he is my Pa.


## The Finest Age

When he was only nine months old,
   And plump and round and pink of cheek,
A joy to tickle and to hold,
   Before he'd even learned to speak,
His gentle mother used to say:
   " It is too bad that he must grow.
If I could only have my way
   His baby ways we'd always know."

And then the year was turned, and he
    Began to toddle round the floor
And name the things that he could see
    And soil the dresses that he wore.
Then many a night she whispered low:
    "Our baby now is such a joy
I hate to think that he must grow
    To be a wild and heedless boy."

But on he went and sweeter grew,
    And then his mother, I recall,
Wished she could keep him always two,
    For that's the finest age of all.
She thought the self-same thing at three,
    And now that he is four, she sighs
To think he cannot always be
    The youngster with the laughing eyes.

Oh, little boy, my wish is not
    Always to keep you four years old.
Each night I stand beside your cot
    And think of what the years may hold;
And looking down on you I pray
    That when we've lost our baby small,
The mother of our man will say
    "This is the finest age of all."

## Out-of-Doors

The kids are out-of-doors once more;
The heavy leggings that they wore,
The winter caps that covered ears
Are put away, and no more tears
Are shed because they cannot go
Until they're bundled up just so.
No more she wonders when they're gone
If they have put their rubbers on;
No longer are they hourly told
To guard themselves against a cold;
Bareheaded now they romp and run
Warmed only by the kindly sun.

She's put their heavy clothes away
And turned the children out to play,
And all the morning long they race
Like madcaps round about the place.
The robins on the fences sing
A gayer song of welcoming,
And seem as though they had a share
In all the fun they're having there.
The wrens and sparrows twitter, too,
A louder and a noisier crew,
As though it pleased them all to see
The youngsters out of doors and free.

Outdoors they scamper to their play
With merry din the livelong day,
And hungrily they jostle in
The favor of the maid to win;
Then, armed with cookies or with cake,
Their way into the yard they make,
And every feathered playmate comes
To gather up his share of crumbs.
The finest garden that I know
Is one where little children grow,
Where cheeks turn brown and eyes are bright,
And all is laughter and delight.

Oh, you may brag of gardens fine,
But let the children race in mine;
And let the roses, white and red,
Make gay the ground whereon they tread.
And who for bloom perfection seeks,
Should mark the color on their cheeks;
No music that the robin spouts
Is equal to their merry shouts;
There is no foliage to compare
With youngsters' sun-kissed, tousled hair:
Spring's greatest joy beyond a doubt
Is when it brings the children out.

## My Paw Said So

Foxes can talk if you know how to listen,
    My Paw said so.
Owls have big eyes that sparkle an' glisten,
    My Paw said so.
Bears can turn flip-flaps an' climb ellum trees,
An' steal all the honey away from the bees,
An' they never mind winter becoz they don't
      freeze;
    My Paw said so.

Girls is a-scared of a snake, but boys ain't,
    My Paw said so.
They holler an' run; an' sometimes they faint,
    My Paw said so.
But boys would be 'shamed to be frightened
      that way
When all that the snake wants to do is to play:
You've got to believe every word that I say,
    My Paw said so.

Wolves ain't so bad if you treat 'em all right,
    My Paw said so.
They're as fond of a game as they are of a fight,
    My Paw said so.
An' all of the animals found in the wood
Ain't always ferocious.  Most times they are
      good.

The trouble is mostly they're misunderstood,
    My Paw said so.


You can think what you like, but I stick to it
        when
    My Paw said so.
An' I'll keep right on sayin', again an' again,
    My Paw said so.
Maybe foxes don't talk to such people as you,
An' bears never show you the tricks they can do,
But I know that the stories I'm tellin' are true,
    My Paw said so.



## A Boy and His Dad

A boy and his dad on a fishing-trip —
There is a glorious fellowship!
Father and son and the open sky
And the white clouds lazily drifting by,
And the laughing stream as it runs along
With the clicking reel like a martial song,
And the father teaching the youngster gay
How to land a fish in the sportsman's way.

I fancy I hear them talking there
In an open boat, and the speech is fair;

And the boy is learning the ways of men
From the finest man in his youthful ken.
Kings, to the youngster, cannot compare
With the gentle father who's with him there.
And the greatest mind of the human race
Not for one minute could take his place.

Which is happier, man or boy?
The soul of the father is steeped in joy,
For he's finding out, to his heart's delight,
That his son is fit for the future fight.
He is learning the glorious depths of him,
And the thoughts he thinks and his every whim,
And he shall discover, when night comes on,
How close he has grown to his little son.

A boy and his dad on a fishing-trip —
Oh, I envy them, as I see them there
Under the sky in the open air,
For out of the old, old long-ago
Come the summer days that I used to know,
When I learned life's truths from my father's
       lips
As I shared the joy of his fishing-trips —
Builders of life's companionship!

# A Boy's Hope for the Future

I'd like to hunt for buffalo an' ride the western
    slope;
I'd like to be a cowboy an' make circles with a
    rope;
I'd like to be a trapper an' sit 'round a fire at
    night
An' hear the wolves an' catamounts a-growling
    at the light.
But buffalo an' catamounts I guess I'll never see,
Coz Pa says that he hopes to make a lawyer out
    of me.

I'd like to be an acrobat, performing in the air,
Pretending I was going to fall to give the folks
    a scare;
I'd like to balance on a pole an' dangle from my
    teeth
An' frighten all the little boys an' girls who sat
    beneath.
But Uncle John, he says he hopes for higher
    things than that,
An' I should have to run away to be an acrobat.

I'd like to be a circus clown an' run around the
    ring
An' wear a funny suit of clothes, an' laugh at
    everything;

I'd like to paint my face all white an' have a lot
of fun,
But Ma says that she must be proud to say that
I'm her son;
She wants to hold her head up high, as high as
it can be,
An' she is hoping she can make a preacher out
of me.

## Couldn't Live Without You

You're just a little fellow with a lot of funny
ways,
Just three-foot-six of mischief set with eyes that
fairly blaze;
You're always up to something with those busy
hands o' yours,
And you leave a trail o' ruin on the walls an' on
the doors,
An' I wonder, as I watch you, an' your curious
tricks I see,
Whatever is the reason that you mean so much
to me.

You're just a chubby rascal with a grin upon
    your face,
Just seven years o' gladness, an' a hard an' try-
    ing case;
You think the world's your playground, an' in
    all you say an' do
You fancy everybody ought to bow an' scrape to
    you;
Dull care's a thing you laugh at just as though
    'twill never be,
So I wonder, little fellow, why you mean so much
    to me.

Now your face is smeared with candy or perhaps
    it's only dirt,
An' it's really most alarming how you tear your
    little shirt;
But I have to smile upon you, an' with all your
    wilful ways,
I'm certain that I need you 'round about me all
    my days;
Yes, I've got to have you with me for somehow
    it's come to be
That I couldn't live without you, for you're all
    the world to me.

# Leader of the Gang

Seems only just a year ago that he was toddling
    round the place
In pretty little colored suits and with a pink
    and shining face.
I used to hold him in my arms to watch when
    our canary sang,
And now to-night he tells me that he's leader
    of his gang.

It seems but yesterday, I vow, that I with fear
    was almost dumb,
Living those dreadful hours of care waiting the
    time for him to come;
And I can still recall the thrill of that first cry
    of his which rang
Within our walls. And now that babe tells me
    he's leader of his gang.

Gone from our lives are all the joys which yes-
    terday we used to own;
The baby that we thought we had, out of the little
    home has flown,
And in his place another stands, whose garments
    in disorder hang,
A lad who now with pride proclaims that he's the
    leader of his gang.

And yet somehow I do not grieve for what it
    seems we may have lost;
To have so strong a boy as this, most cheerfully
    I pay the cost.
I find myself a sense of joy to comfort every
    little pang,
And pray that they shall find in him a worthy
    leader of the gang.


## Little Girls Are Best

Little girls are mighty nice,
    Take 'em any way they come;
They are always worth their price;
    Life without 'em would be glum;
Run earth's lists of treasures through,
    Pile 'em high until they fall,
Gold an' costly jewels, too —
    Little girls are best of all.

Nothing equals 'em on earth!
    I'm an old man an' I know
Any little girl is worth
    More than all the gold below;

Eyes o' blue or brown or gray,
  Raven hair or golden curls,
There's no joy on earth to-day
  Quite so fine as little girls.

Pudgy nose or freckled face,
  Fairy-like or plain to see,
God has surely blessed the place
  Where a little girl may be;
They're the jewels of His crown
  Dropped to earth from heaven above,
Like wee angel souls sent down
  To remind us of His love.

God has made some lovely things —
  Roses red an' skies o' blue,
Trees an' babbling silver springs,
  Gardens glistening with dew —
But take every gift to man,
  Big an' little, great an' small,
Judge it on its merits, an'
  Little girls are best of all!

## What Home's Intended For

When the young folks gather 'round in the good
    old-fashioned way,
Singin' all the latest songs gathered from the
    newest play,
Or they start the phonograph an' shove the chairs
    back to the wall
An' hold a little party dance, I'm happiest of all.
Then I sorter settle back, plumb contented to the
    core,
An' I tell myself most proudly, that's what
    home's intended for.

When the laughter's gaily ringin' an' the room is
    filled with song,
I like to sit an' watch 'em, all that glad an' merry
    throng,
For the ragtime they are playin' on the old piano
    there
Beats any high-toned music where the bright
    lights shine an' glare,
An' the racket they are makin' stirs my pulses
    more and more,
So I whisper in my gladness: that's what home's
    intended for.

Then I smile an' say to Mother, let 'em move the
    chairs about,
Let 'em frolic in the parlor, let 'em shove the
    tables out,
Jus' so long as they are near us, jus' so long as
    they will stay
By the fireplace we are keepin', harm will never
    come their way,
An' you'll never hear me grumble at the bills that
    keep me poor,
It's the finest part o' livin' — that's what home's
    intended for.

### *Aw Gee Whiz!*

Queerest little chap he is,
Always saying: " Aw Gee Whiz! "
Needing something from the store
That you've got to send him for
And you call him from his play,
Then it is you hear him say:
    " Aw Gee Whiz! "

Seems that most expressive phrase
Is a part of childhood days;
Call him in at supper time,
Hands and face all smeared with grime,
Send him up to wash, and he
Answers you disgustedly:
    "Aw Gee Whiz!"

When it's time to go to bed
And he'd rather play instead,
As you call him from the street,
He comes in with dragging feet,
Knowing that he has to go,
Then it is he mutters low:
    "Aw Gee Whiz!"

Makes no difference what you ask
Of him as a little task;
He has yet to learn that life
Crosses many a joy with strife,
So when duty mars his play,
Always we can hear him say:
    "Aw Gee Whiz!"

# The Living Beauties

I never knew, until they went,
How much their laughter really meant.
I never knew how much the place
Depended on each little face;
How barren home could be and drear
Without its living beauties here.

I never knew that chairs and books
Could wear such sad and solemn looks!
That rooms and halls could be at night
So still and drained of all delight.
This home is now but brick and board
Where bits of furniture are stored.

I used to think I loved each shelf
And room for what it was itself.
And once I thought each picture fine
Because I proudly called it mine.
But now I know they mean no more
Than art works hanging in a store.

Until they went away to roam
I never knew what made it home.
But I have learned that all is base,
However wonderful the place
And decked with costly treasures rare,
Unless the living joys are there.

## Story Telling

Most every night when they're in bed,
And both their little prayers have said,
They shout for me to come upstairs
And tell them tales of grizzly bears,
And Indians and gypsies bold,
And eagles with the claws that hold
A baby's weight, and fairy sprites
That roam the woods on starry nights.

And I must illustrate these tales,
Must imitate the northern gales
That toss the Indian's canoe,
And show the way he paddles, too.
If in the story comes a bear,
I have to pause and sniff the air
And show the way he climbs the trees
To steal the honey from the bees.

And then I buzz like angry bees
And sting him on his nose and knees
And howl in pain, till mother cries:
"That pair will never shut their eyes,
While all that noise up there you make;
You're simply keeping them awake."
And then they whisper: "Just one more,"
And once again I'm forced to roar.

New stories every night they ask,
And that is not an easy task;
I have to be so many things:
The frog that croaks, the lark that sings,
The cunning fox, the frightened hen;
But just last night they stumped me, when
They wanted me to twist and squirm
And imitate an angleworm.

At last they tumble off to sleep,
And softly from their room I creep
And brush and comb the shock of hair
I tossed about to be a bear.
Then mother says: "Well, I should say
You're just as much a child as they."
But you can bet I'll not resign
That story-telling job of mine.

# The World and Bud

If we were all alike, what a dreadful world
    'twould be!
No one would know which one was you or which
    of us was me.
We'd never have a " Skinny " or a " Freckles "
    or a " Fat,"
An' there wouldn't be a sissy boy to wear a
    velvet hat;
An' we'd all of us be pitchers when we played
    a baseball match,
For we'd never have a feller who'd have nerve
    enough to catch.

If we were all alike an' looked an' thought the
    same,
I wonder how'd they call us, 'cause there'd only
    be one name.
An' there'd only be one flavor for our ice cream
    sodas, too,
An' one color for a necktie an' I 'spose that
    would be blue;
An' maybe we'd have mothers who were very
    fond of curls,
An' they'd make us fellers wear our hair like
    lovely little girls.

Sometimes I think it's funny when I hear some
    feller say
That he isn't fond of chocolate, when I eat it
    every day.
Or some other fellow doesn't like the books I
    like to read;
But I'm glad that we are different, yes, siree! I
    am indeed.
If everybody looked alike an' talked alike, Oh,
    Gee!
We'd never know which one was you or which
    of us was me.


## The Choir Boy

They put his spotless surplice on
    And tied his flowing tie,
And he was fair to look upon
    As he went singing by.
He sang the hymns with gentle grace,
    That little lad of nine,
For there was something in his face
    Which seemed almost divine.

His downcast eye was good to see,
  His brow was smooth and fair,
And no one dreamed that there could be
  A rascal plotting there;
Yet when all heads in prayer were bowed,
  God's gracious care to beg,
The boy next to him cried aloud:
  "Quit pinching o' my leg!"

A pious little child he seemed,
  An angel born to sing;
Beholding him, none ever dreamed
  He'd do a naughty thing;
Yet many a sudden "ouch!" proclaimed
  That he had smuggled in
For mischief-making, unashamed,
  A most disturbing pin.

And yet, I think, from high above,
  The Father looking down,
Knows everything he's thinking of
  And smiles when mortals frown,
For in the spotless surplice white
  Which is his mother's joy,
He knows he's not an angel bright,
  But just a healthy boy.

## To the Little Baby

You know your mother — that's plain as day,
But those wide blue eyes of you seem to say
When I bend over your crib: "Now who
Are you?"
It's little figure I cut, I know,
And faces trouble a baby so,
But I'm the gladdest of all the glad —
Your dad!

You're two months old, and you see us smile,
And I know you are wondering all the while
Whoever on earth can these people be
You see.
You've learned your mother; you know her well
When hunger rattles the dinner bell,
But somehow or other you cannot place
My face.

As yet, I'm but one of the passing throng,
The curious people who come along
And pause at your crib, and you seem to say
Each day:
"I know one voice that is sweet to hear,
I know her step when my mother's near,
I know her wonderful smile — but who
Are you?"

"You always come with the same old grin,
Your finger's rough when you tickle my chin,

But you run away when I start to cry,
And I
Don't understand when visitors call
Why you're so afraid they will let me fall.
You are the queerest of all the queer
Folks here!"

It's true that over your crib I stand
And tickle your chin with my rough old hand
And I run away when you start to cry,
But I
Have a right to my queer little funny ways,
To boast your worth and to sound your praise,
For I am the gladdest of all the glad —
Your dad.

## Pretending Not to See

Sometimes at the table, when
He gets misbehavin', then
Mother calls across to me:
"Look at him, now!  Don't you see
What he's doin', sprawlin' there!
Make him sit up in his chair.
Don't you see the messy way
That he's eating?"  An' I say:
"No.  He seems all right just now.
What's he doing anyhow?"

Mother placed him there by me,
An' she thinks I ought to see

Every time he breaks the laws
An' correct him, just because
There will come a time some day
When he mustn't act that way.
But I can't be all along
Scoldin' him for doin' wrong.
So if something goes astray,
I jus' look the other way.

Mother tells me now an' then
I'm the easiest o' men,
An' in dealin' with the lad
I will never see the bad
That he does, an' I suppose
Mother's right for Mother knows;
But I'd hate to feel that I'm
Here to scold him all the time.
Little faults might spoil the day,
So I look the other way.

Look the other way an' try
Not to let him catch my eye,
Knowin' all the time that he
Doesn't mean so bad to be;
Knowin', too, that now an' then
I am not the best o' men;
Hopin', too, the times I fall
That the Father of us all,
Lovin', watchin' over me,
Will pretend He doesn't see.

## The Fairy and the Robin

A fairy and a robin met
Beside a bed of mignonette.
The robin bowed and raised his hat,
And smiled a smile as wide as — that —
Then said: " Miss Fairy, I declare,
I'd kiss you, only I don't dare."

The fairy curtsied low and said:
" Your breast is such a lovely red,
And you are such a handsome thing,
And, oh, such pretty songs you sing —
I'd gladly kiss you now, but I
May only kiss a butterfly."

The robin spoke a silly word:
" I'm sorry I was born a bird!
Were I a fairy-man instead,
Then you and I might some day wed."
The fairy laughed and said: " My dear,
God had to have some robins here.

" Be glad you're what you are and sing
And cheer the people in the Spring.
I play with children as I'm told,
But you bring joy to young and old,
And it seems always strange to me
I'm one the old folks never see."

The robin spoke: "Perhaps it's best.
I'll sing my songs and show my breast
And be a robin, and you stay
And share in all the children's play.
God needs us both, so let us try
To do our duty — you and I."

How do I know they said these things?
I saw the robin spread his wings,
I saw the fairy standing up
Upon a golden buttercup,
I hid myself behind a wall
And listened close and heard it all.

## The Spoiler

With a twinkle in his eye
He'd come gayly walkin' by
An' he'd whistle to the children
    An' he'd beckon 'em to come,
Then he'd chuckle low an' say,
"Come along, I'm on my way,
An' it's I that need your company
    To buy a little gum."

When his merry call they'd hear,
All the children, far an' near,
Would come flyin' from the gardens
   Like the chickens after wheat;
When we'd shake our heads an' say:
" No, you mustn't go to-day ! "
He'd beg to let him have 'em
   In a pack about his feet.

Oh, he spoiled 'em, one an' all;
There was not a youngster small
But was over-fed on candy
   An' was stuffed with lollypops,
An' I think his greatest joy
Was to get some girl or boy
An' bring 'em to their parents
   All besmeared by chocolate drops.

Now the children's hearts are sore
For he comes to them no more,
And no more to them he whistles
   And no more for them he stops;
But in Paradise, I think,
With his chuckle and his wink,
He is leading little angels
   To the heavenly candy shops.

## High Chair Days

High chair days are the best of all,
 Or so they seem to me,
Days when tumbler and platter fall
 And the King smiles merrily;
When the regal arms and the regal feet
A constant patter of music beat,
And the grown-ups bow in a gracious way
To the high chair monarch who rules the day.

High chair days, and the throne not dressed
 In golden or purple hues
But an old style thing, let it be confessed,
 His grandmother used to use;
Its legs are scarred and a trifle bowed,
But the king who sits on the chair is proud,
And he throws his rattle and silver cup
For the joy of making us pick them up.

The old high chair in the dining room
 Is a handsomer thing by far
Than the costly chairs in the lonely gloom
 Of the childless mansions are,

For the sweetest laughter the world has known
Comes day by day from that humble throne,
And the happiest tables, morn and night,
Have a high chair placed at the mother's right.

The old high chair is a joy sublime,
    Yet it brings us its hour of pain,
For we've put it away from time to time,
    Perhaps never to need again;
Yet God was good, and the angles tapped,
And again was the old high chair unwrapped,
And proud was I when I heard the call
To bring it back to the dining hall.

There are griefs to meet and cares to face
    Through the years that lie ahead;
The proudest monarch must lose his place
    And lie with the splendid dead;
I know there are blows I shall have to meet,
I must pay with the bitter for all life's sweet,
But I live in dread of that coming day
When forever the high chair goes away.

# Rich

Who has a troop of romping youth
  About his parlor floor,
Who nightly hears a round of cheers,
  When he is at the door,
Who is attacked on every side
  By eager little hands
That reach to tug his grizzled mug,
  The wealth of earth commands.

Who knows the joys of girls and boys,
  His lads and lassies, too,
Who's pounced upon and bounced upon
  When his day's work is through,
Whose trousers know the gentle tug
  Of some glad little tot,
The baby of his crew of love,
  Is wealthier than a lot.

Oh, be he poor and sore distressed
  And weary with the fight,
If with a whoop his healthy troop
  Run, welcoming at night,
And kisses greet him at the end
  Of all his toiling grim,
With what is best in life he's blest
  And rich men envy him.

## Dirty Hands

I have to wash myself at night before I go to bed,
An' wash again when I get up, an' wash before
    I'm fed,
An' Ma inspects my neck an' ears an' Pa my
    hands an' shirt —
They seem to wonder why it is that I'm so fond
    of dirt.
But Bill — my chum — an' I agree that we have
    never seen
A feller doing anything whose hands were white
    an' clean.

Bill's mother scolds the same as mine an' calls
    him in from play
To make him wash his face an' hands a dozen
    times a day.
Dirt seems to worry mothers so.  But when the
    plumber comes
To fix the pipes, it's plain to see he never scrubs
    his thumbs;
His clothes are always thick with grease, his face
    is smeared with dirt,
An' he is not ashamed to show the smudges on
    his shirt.

The motorman who runs the car has hands much
    worse than mine,

An' I have noticed when we ride there's dirt in
    every line.
The carpenter who works around our house can
    mend a chair
Or put up shelves or fix the floor, an' mother
    doesn't care
That he's not in his Sunday best; she never
    interferes
An' makes him stop his work to go upstairs to
    wash his ears.

The fellers really doing things, as far as I can see,
Have hands and necks an' ears that are as dirty
    as can be.
The man who fixes father's car when he can't
    make it go,
Most always has a smudgy face — his hands
    aren't white as snow.
But I must wash an' wash an' wash while every-
    body knows
The most important men in town have dirty
    hands an' clo'es.

# INDEX OF FIRST LINES

A boy and his dad on a fishing trip........ 159
A boy and his dog make a glorious pair.... 65
A fairy and a robin met.................. 179
A little ship goes out to sea.............. 76
Always whenever I want to play.......... 150
A smudge on his nose and a smear on his
  cheek ................................ 44
At sixteen months, when they start to walk 45

Come back you little feller............... 33
Comes in flying from the street.......... 49

Down the lanes of boyhood............. 39

Each evening on my lap there climbs..... 131
Every night she runs to me............. 112

First thing in the morning............. 88
Folks are queer as they can be.......... 144
Foxes can talk if you know how to listen 158

Give me the house where the toys are
  strewn ................................ 73
God made the little girls for fun......... 82
Got a sliver in my hand................. 61

Habits are things which you do an' you
  shouldn't ............................. 15
He is just a boy with eyes aglow......... 18
Her tears are very near to-day.......... 23
He's supposed to be our son............. 32
High chair days are the best of all...... 182

I'd like to hunt for buffalo............. 161
I don't mind lickin's now and then...... 85

I don't see why Pa likes him so.......... 118
If I could have my wish to-night........ 109
If we were all alike..................... 173
I hadn't asked about it for a week or two  41
I have to wash myself at night.......... 185
I know a wonderful land, I said........... 126
I know what makes a Grandma grand....  13
I like 'em in the winter when their cheeks
   are slightly pale.......................  58
I like to get to thinking of the old days that
   are gone.............................  59
I'm sorry for a feller if he hasn't any aunt 104
I'm the bumps and bruises doctor........ 141
I never knew until they went............ 170
I reckon the finest sight of all............. 108
In the corner she's left the mechanical toy  98
I've seen some lovely sights, I think......  37
I saw him in the distance................ 142
It's funny, 'bout a feller's hat............ 149
I want my boy to love his home..........  50
I wish I would get sick and couldn't go..  20
I wisht my pa would ast me to..........  26
I would rather be the daddy.............  72

Last night I got to thinkin'.............. 120
Last night she hurried out to say........  24
Last night the baby cried.  And I........  75
Last year he wanted building blocks...... 113
Little girls are mighty nice.............. 165
Little sticky fingers, it is very plain to see  35
Little women, little men.................. 128

Ma says no, it's too much care............ 137
Most every night when they're in bed.... 171
My father says that I ought to be........  99
My grandpa is the finest man............ 115

No children in the house to play......... 145
Now, children, if you will just gather about 21

Oh, little girl with eyes of brown......... 147
Once there was a boy who never........ 153
One day the doctor came................. 96

Queerest little chap he is................. 168

Seems only just a year ago that he was
  toddling .............................. 164
She is gentle, kind and fair............. 77
Sit here on my knee, little girl, and I'll tell 47
Some day the world will need a man...... 56
Some folks pray for a boy, and some....... 66
Something to talk about, something to do 31
Sometimes at the table.................. 177
Sometimes I'm almost glad to hear....... 93

Tain't nothin' to laugh at as I can see.... 69
Teach the children of the Flag........... 71
Tell me, what is half so sweet........... 46
Tell us a story, comes the cry........... 123
There are little eyes upon you........... 91
The children bring us laughter........... 90
The first few weeks she never knew...... 11
The golden dreamboat's ready, all her silken
  sails ................................. 54
The kids are out-of-doors once more...... 156
The kids at our house number three....... 106
The other night 'bout two o'clock........ 79
The path o' little children is the path I want
  to tread .............................. 16
There is sorrow in the household......... 130
There may be happier times than this.... 102
There's a bump on his brow and a smear
  on his cheek.......................... 81

There's a little chap at our house that is
being mighty good...................... 63
There's a little house on humble street.... 27
There's a new little Gimme at our house.. 19
There was a bear — his name was Jim.... 133
The train of cars that Santa brought...... 117
They come to my room at the break of day 86
They put his spotless surplice on......... 174
Tuggin' at your bottle................... 83
Twenty times a day we go............... 42

Up to the ceiling....................... 138

"Wait till your Pa comes home!" Oh, dear! 67
We've got another mouth to feed......... 125
What's the matter with you — ain't I al-
ways been your friend?................ 53
When a little baby dies.................. 52
Whenever I come where the old folks is.. 38
When father couldn't wear them......... 111
When he was only nine months old...... 154
When Pa comes home, I'm at the door... 135
"When shall I be a man?" he said........ 139
When there's company for tea............ 152
When the young folks gather round...... 167
When we wuz kids together, an' we didn't
have a care........................... 29
Who has a troop of romping youth....... 184
With a twinkle in his eye............... 180
With time our notions allus change...... 94
World wide over this is said............. 101

You know your mother — that's plain as
day ................................... 176
You're just a little fellow............... 162
"You're spoilin' them!" the mother cries... 122

# *For your reading pleasure...*